Caroline Bowles Southey

The Poetical Works of Caroline Bowles Southey

Collected Edition

Caroline Bowles Southey

The Poetical Works of Caroline Bowles Southey
Collected Edition

ISBN/EAN: 9783337312626

Printed in Europe, USA, Canada, Australia, Japan

Cover: Foto ©Thomas Meinert / pixelio.de

More available books at **www.hansebooks.com**

THE POETICAL WORKS

OF

CAROLINE BOWLES SOUTHEY

COLLECTED EDITION

WILLIAM BLACKWOOD AND SONS
EDINBURGH AND LONDON
MDCCCLXVII

CONTENTS.

	PAGE
THE BIRTHDAY	1
THE LEGEND OF SANTAREM	97
THE PAUPER'S DEATHBED	102
SONNET.—1818	103
CONTE A MON CHIEN	104
SUFFICIENT UNTO THE DAY IS THE EVIL THEREOF	116
FAREWELL TO MY FRIENDS	122
TO A DYING INFANT	124
MY OLD DOG AND I	128
RANGER'S GRAVE	133
THE MARINER'S HYMN	135
SONNET	136
THE BROKEN BRIDGE	137
SONNET	144
THE LADYE'S BRYDALLE	145
TO MY BIRDIE	155
TO MY OLD CANARY	157
TO THE MEMORY OF ISABEL SOUTHEY	163
SONNET	164

Contents.

THERE IS A TONGUE IN EVERY LEAF	165
ON THE NEAR PROSPECT OF LEAVING HOME.—1818	167
AUTUMN FLOWERS	168
TO DEATH	170
ONCE UPON A TIME	171
THAT'S WHAT WE ARE	174
DEPARTURE	180
THE CHILD'S UNBELIEF	181
THE GREENWOOD SHRIFT	184
THE WARNING	188
THE THREE FRIENDS	190
MY GARDEN	191
THE YOUNG GREY HEAD	197
LITTLE LEONARD'S "GOOD-NIGHT"	209
HOW SWIFT IS A GLANCE OF THE MIND!	210
ON THE REMOVAL OF SOME FAMILY PORTRAITS	212
SONNET.—1818	215
WILD FLOWERS	216
TO LITTLE MARY	220
SONNET.—1821	222
THE LEGEND OF THE LIDO	223
THE RIVER	233
SUNDAY EVENING	234
THE CHURCHYARD	237
TO THE SWEET-SCENTED CYCLAMEN	239
THE WELCOME HOME.—1820	243
THE DEATH OF THE FLOWERS	246
WHEN SHALL WE MEET AGAIN?	247

Contents.

THE LANDING OF THE PRIMROSE	248
THE DYING MOTHER TO HER INFANT	252
THE LAST JOURNEY	256
THE SPELL OF MUSIC	259
TOO LATE	260
THE EVENING WALK	262
'TIS HARD TO DIE IN SPRING	276
LAMENT FOR LILIAS	277
THE NIGHT-SMELLING STOCK	279
PAST AND PRESENT	282
THE WINTRY MAY.—1837	283
I WEEP, BUT NOT REBELLIOUS TEARS	285
IT IS NOT DEATH	286
ABJURATION	288
ONCE UPON A TIME	291
I NEVER CAST A FLOWER AWAY	292
A FAIR PLACE AND PLEASANT	293
MY EVENING	294
THE PRIMROSE	300
ARCHBISHOP GERSON	301
NOTES TO "THE BIRTHDAY"	304

POEMS.

---o---

THE BIRTHDAY.

PART THE FIRST.

CONTENTS.

The Sixth of December.—The Family Circle.—The Old Nurse.—The First Sorrow.—Education.—Drawing.—The Landscape.—Parental Hopes.—Cutting-out.—Dolls.—Needlework.—Fairy Sports.—The First Writing-Lesson.—Solitary Childhood.—The Garden.—Spring.

DARK gloomy day of Winter's darkest month!
Scarce through the lowering sky your dawning light
In one pale watery streak breaks feebly forth.
No sunbeam through that congregated mass
Of heavy rolling clouds will pierce to-day.
Beams of the cheering sun! I court ye not.
Best with the saddened temper of my soul
Accords the pensive stillness Nature wears;
For Memory, with a serious reckoning, now
Is busy with the past—with other years,

The Birthday.

When the return of this, my natal day,
Brought gladness to warm hearts that loved me well.
As wayworn Pilgrim on the last hill-top
Lingers awhile, and, leaning on his staff,
Looks back upon the pleasant plain o'erpast,
Retracing far, with retrospective eye,
The course of every little glancing stream
And winding valley path, late hurried o'er,
Perchance, with careless unobservant eye,
Fixed on some distant point of fairer promise—
As with long pause the highest summit gained—
Dividing, like the Tyrolean ridge,
Summer from winter,—that wayfaring man
Leans on his staff, and looks a long farewell
To all the lovely land: So linger I,
Life's lonely Pilgrim, on the last hill-top,
With thoughtful, tender, retrospective gaze,
Ere, turning, down the deep descent I go,
Of the cold shadowy side.
                              Fair sunbright scene!
Not sunny all—ah, no!—I love to dwell,
Seeking repose and rest, on that green track,
Your farthest verge, along whose primrose path
Danced happy Childhood, hand in hand with Joy,
And dove-eyed Innocence—unawakened yet
Their younger sister Hope—while flowers sprang up
Printing the fairy footseps as they passed.
Return, ye golden hours! old times! return:
Even ye, ye simple pleasures, I invoke,
With rose-hues tinting life's delightful dawn!
Yes, I invoke ye, dear departed days!
I call ye from the land of shadows back,
Mellowed by softening Time, but not obscured,
Distinct in twilight beauty, such as steals,

The Birthday.

Like grey-robed Vestal in some pageant's train,
With slow advance on sunset's crimson wake.

Come in your mellowed hues, long vanished years!
Come in your softened outline, passing slow
O'er the charmed mirror, as I gaze entranced—
There first I see, when struggling into life,
Dawned the first ray of infant consciousness;
There first I see a tender, watchful group,
Hailing delightfully that token faint.
Two Parents then, inestimable wealth!
Two Parents me, their only darling, blessed:
And one—the good, the gentle, the beloved!—
My Mother's Mother. Still methinks I see
Her gracious countenance. The unruffled brow,
The soft blue eye, the still carnationed cheek
Unwrinkled yet, though sixty passing years
Of light and shade—ah! deeply shaded some—
Had streaked with silvery grey her tresses fair.
Even now methinks that placid smile I see,
That kindly beamed on all, but chief on me,
Her age's darling! Nor of hers alone:
One yet surviving in a green old age,
Her Mother lived; and, when I saw the light,
Rejoicing hailed her daughter's daughter's child.

Nor from that kindred patriarchal group
Be thou excluded, long-tried humble friend!
Old faithful Servant! Sole survivor now
Of those beloved, for whom thine aged hands
The last sad service tremblingly performed,
That closed their eyes, and for the long, long sleep
Arrayed them in the vestments of the grave.
Yes, THOU survivest still to tend and watch

Me, the sad orphan of thy Master's house!
My cradle hast thou rocked; with patient love,
Love all enduring, all indulgent, borne
My childhood's wayward fancies, that from thee
Never rebuke or frown encountered cold.

* * * * * *

Come nearer.—Let me rest my cheek even now
On thy dear shoulder, printed with a mark
Indelible of suffering borne for me:
Fruit of contagious contact long endured,
When on that pillow lay my infant head
For days and nights, a helpless dying weight,
So thought by all; as almost all but thee
Shrank from the little victim of a scourge
Yet uncontrolled by Jenner's heaven-taught hand.
And with my growth has grown the debt of love;
For many a day beside my restless bed,
In later years thy station hast thou kept,
Watching my slumbers, or with fondest wiles
Soothing the fretful, feverish hour of pain:
And when at last, with languid frame I rose,
Feeble as infancy, what hand like thine,
With such a skilful gentleness, performed
The handmaid's office?—tenderly, as when
A helpless babe thou oft hadst robed me thus.
Oh, the vast debt!—yet to my grateful heart
Not burdensome, not irksome to repay:
For small requital dost thou claim, dear Nurse!
Only to know thy fondly lavished cares
Have sometimes power to cheer and comfort me:
Then in thy face reflected, beams the light,
The unwonted gladness, that irradiates mine.
Long mayst thou sit as now, invited oft,
Beside my winter fire, with busy hands

The Birthday.

And polished needles knitting the warm wool;
Or resting with meek reverence from thy work,
When from *that Book*, that blessèd Book! I read
The words of Truth and Life,—thy hope and mine.

There shalt thou oft, Time's faithful chronicler!
Tell o'er to my unwearied ear old tales
Of days and things that were—and are no more.
Yes, thou shalt tell, with what a noble air,
On wedding, or on christening festival,
The portly form of my Granduncle moved;
In what fair waving folds the snowy lawn,
Bordered with costly point, redundant flowed,
Beneath his goodly amplitude of chin;
And how magnificent in rich brocade,
And broidered rosebuds, and rough woven gold,
Half-down his thigh the long flapped waistcoat fell.
A comely raiment! that might put to shame
The shrunken garb of these degenerate days.
Then shall I hear enumeration proud
Of female glories—silks that "stood on end!"
Tabbies and damasks, and rich Paduasoys,
And flowing sacks, and full-trimmed negligees,
And petticoats whose gorgeous panoply,
Stiffened with whalebone ribs the circuit vast,
With independent grandeur stood sublime.

Describe again, while I attend well pleased,
That ancient manor of my Norman race,
In all its feudal greatness: In *thy* time,
Of simple girlhood, to thy wondering mind,
Still most magnificent, nor yet forsaken
By the "old family." The ancient gateway
Surmounted by heraldic sculpture proud;

The Birthday.

The round tower dovecote with its thousand holes—
Seignorial right, with jealous care maintained—
And my Great-grandam with her stately presence—
I mind it well—among her maidens throned
At the eternal tapestry. I smile;—
But more, good sooth! in sadness than in mirth.
I've seen the ancient gateway where it stands
An isolated arch. The noble trees,
A triple avenue, its proud approach,
Gone as they ne'er had been; the dovecote tower
A desecrated ruin; the old house——
Dear Nurse! full fain am I to weep with thee
The faded glories of "the good old time."

Return, digressive Fancy! Maiden mild
Of the dark dreamy eye, pale Memory!
Uphold again the glass, reflecting late
My happy self in happy childhood's dawn,
By that dear guardian group encircled close.

Already changed!—already clouded o'er
With the Death-shadow that fair morning sky—
The kindred band is broken. One goes hence,
The very aged. Follows soon, too soon,
Another most endeared, the next in age.
Then fell from childhood's eyes the earliest tears
Shed for Man's penal doom. Unconscious half,
Incomprehensive of the awful truth;
But flowing faster, when I looked around
And saw that others wept; and faster still,
When clinging round my Nurse's neck, with face
Half-buried there, to hide the bursting grief,
I heard her tell how in the churchyard cold,
In the dark pit, the form I loved was laid.

The Birthday.

Bitter exceedingly the passionate grief
That wrings to agony the infant heart:
The *first* sharp sorrow:—ay, the breaking up
Of that deep fountain, never to be sealed,
Till we with Time close up the great account.
But that first outbreak, by its own excess
Exhausted soon; exhausting the young powers:
The quivering lip relaxes into smiles,
As soothing slumber, softly stealing on;
Less and less frequent comes the swelling sob,
Till like a summer breeze it dies away;
While on the silken eyelash, and the cheek
Flushed into crimson, hang the large round drops—
Well I remember, from that storm of grief
Diverted soon, with what sensations new
Of female vanity—inherent sin!
I saw myself arrayed in mourning frock
And long crape sash——Oh, many a riper grief
Forgets itself as soon before a glass
Reflecting the becomingness of weeds!

Soon came the days when fond parental care
'Gan mingle easy tasks with childish play.
Right welcome lessons! conned with willing mind:
For it was told me, by such labour won,
And exercise of patience, I should gain
Access to countless treasures hid in books.
"What! shall I read myself, and *when I will*,
All those fine stories Jane can tell sometimes
When she's good-natured?—but not half so well—
Oh, no! not half—as Cousin Marianne.
What! shall I read about the sea of glass
The lady walked on to the ivory hill?
And all about those children at the well

The Birthday.

That met the fairy, and the toads, and frogs,
And diamonds; and about the talking bird,
And dancing water, and the singing bough,
And Princess Fairstar?   Shall I read all that,
And more, and *when I will*, in printed books?
Oh, let me learn!"—And never student's brain,
Fagging for college prize, or straining hard,
In prospect of tremendous little go,
To fetch up Time's leeway in idlesse lost,
Applied with such intensity as mine.

And soon attained, and sweet the fruit I reaped.
Oh, never ending, ever new delight!
Stream swelling still to meet the eager lip!
Receiving as it flows fresh gushing rills
From hidden sources, purer, more profound.
Parents! dear parents! if the latent powers
Called into action by your early cares—
God's blessing on them!—had attained no more
Than that acquaintance with His written will,
Your first most pious purpose to instil,
How could I e'er acquit me of a debt
Might bankrupt Gratitude?   If scant my stores
Of human learning;—to my mother tongues,
A twofold heritage, wellnigh confined
My skill in languages;—if adverse Fate—
Heathenish phrase!—if *Providence* has fixed
Barriers impassable 'cross many a path
Anticipation with her Hope-winged feet,
Youthfully buoyant, all undoubting trod;—
If in the mind's infirmity, erewhile,
Thoughts that are almost murmurs whisper low
Stinging comparisons, suggestions sad,
Of what I *am*, and what I *might have* been—

The Birthday.

This Earth, so wide and glorious! I fast bound,
A human lichen, to one narrow spot—
A sickly, worthless weed! Such brave bright spirits,
Starring this nether sphere, and I—lone wretch!
Cut off from oral intercourse with all—
" The day far spent," and oh, how little known!—
The night at hand, alas! and nothing done ;—
And neither "word, nor knowledge, nor device,
Nor wisdom, in the grave whereto I go."

* * * * * *

When thoughts like these arise, permitted tests,
Proving my frailty, and Thy mercy, Lord,
Let but Thy ministering angel draw mine eyes
To yonder *Book;* and, lo! this troublous world
Fades from before me like a morning mist,
And, in a spirit *not* mine own, I cry,
" Perish all knowledge but what leads to Thee !"

And, was it chance, or thy prevailing taste,
Beloved instructress! that selected first,
Part of my daily task, a portion short,
Culled from thy ' Seasons,' Thomson?—Happy choice,
Howe'er directed, happy choice for me!
For as I read, new thoughts, new images,
Thrilled through my heart with undefined delight,
Awakening so th' incipient elements
Of tastes and sympathies that with my life
Have grown and strengthened; often on its course,
Yea, on its darkest moments, shedding soft
That rich warm glow they only can impart—
A sensibility to Nature's charms
That seems its living spirit to infuse,
A breathing soul, in things inanimate,
To hold communion with the stirring air,

The breath of flowers, the ever-shifting clouds,
The rustling leaves, the music of the stream,
To people solitude with airy shapes,
And the dark hour, when Night and Silence reigns,
With immaterial forms of other worlds ;
But best and noblest privilege, to feel
Pervading Nature's all-harmonious whole,
The Great Creator's presence, in His works.

Those happy evenings, when, on seat high raised,
By ponderous folio, placed on cushioned chair
Close to the table drawn, with candles snuffed,
And outspread paper, and long pencil, shaved
To finest point—to my unpractised hand
Not trusted yet the sharply dangerous knife,
Like all forbidden things, most coveted—
Oh, blissful hour! when thus installed on high,
In fulness of enjoyment, shapes uncouth,
Chaotic groups, I traced. The first attempt,
Two crooked strokes, that, nodding inward, prop
A fellow pair—a transverse parallel.
The *House* thus roofed, behold from either end
Tall chimneys twain sprout up like asses' ears,
From which, as from a fiery forge beneath,
Ascend huge volumed smoke-wreaths to the sky.
Next in the stately front, strokes—one—two—three ;
There gaps the door, as wide as half the house,
And thick on either hand come cross-barred squares,
Hight windows, that for number would tire out
The patience of that keenly prying wight,
The tax-collector; while from one, be sure,
Looks out some favourite form of absent friend,
Whose house that goodly fabric represents.
Close on each side, two poles, surmounted high

The Birthday.

By full round wigs, assume the name of trees;
And up the road, that widens farthest off,
In brave contempt of stiff perspective rule,
Comes coach-and-six, containing—who *but me*,
And *all* my friends, to visit that fine house!
Then follow man and horse—a gallant steed,
With legs, and mane, and tail, and all complete,—
The rider so secure upon his back,
He need but stretch his legs, and touch the ground.
Thick flies the dust—out flies the brandished whip—
On, on they go; and if they reach the house,
That horseman tall may take it on his palm.
As erst Glumdalclitch handled Gulliver.
And now a five-barred gate, and sundry pales,
And up aloft a flight of birds, so huge
They must be cranes at least, migrating hence;
Some cocks and hens before the door convened—
A dog and cat, and pig with curly tail,
And lo! the *Landscape* in all parts complete!

And never artist of the olden time,
Renowned Lorraine, or wonder-working Cuyp,
Or he, the mighty genius of the storm,
Sublime Salvator, on his masterpiece
Such looks of sweet complacency bestowed
As I on mine. And other eyes beheld,
As pleased, as partial; and parental hearts
From the bewildered and incongruous maze
Sweet inference drew of future excellence,
Saw combination in the motley whole,
Conceptions picturesque in crooked strokes,
And taste and genius manifest throughout.
Discernment keen! that with excursive eye
Pierces the dark dropped curtain, wisely dropped!

That shrouds futurity. As he of old,
The fated Goth, in that Toledan cave
Saw shadowed out, "as in a glass revealed,"
Things uncreated yet, that were to be;
But he beheld the downfall of his hopes,
His line extinct, his empire overthrown.
Appalling vision! type of woes foredoomed—
Far fairer that, less faithfully fulfilled,
The pageant that in long perspective view
Reveals, undoubted, to a parent's eye
The future glories of his infant race—
He, while the fairy people round his chair
Hold their gay revel, from the mimic sport
Auspicious omen draws, and sage portent.

That fair, bold boy, with high undaunted brow,
And broad white chest and shoulders, who bestrides
His father's cane—a gallant war-horse feigned,
Himself the warlike rider, and with shout
And brandished arm, and voice of proud command,
Marshals his legions—chairs and cushions ranged
In rank and file—and prances round the room,
The valiant leader of that well-trained host;—
Is not the future hero manifest,
The laurelled victor, in that noble boy?
And he, with curly pate and bright black eyes,
And dimpled mouth of arch significance—
He ever ready with his "quips and cranks,"
And shifts, and windings, and keen subterfuge,
Detected misdemeanour to excuse,
Averting dexterous the suspended rod—
Already fancy hears that prating tongue,
Subtle, ingenious, disputatious, bold,
The organ of a future barrister;

Or round that chubby face, with prouder hope,
Adjusts an awful majesty of wig:
Lo! on that cushion, where he sits sublime
(His woolsack now), the future Chancellor.
That gentle child, with pale transparent cheek,
And large mild eyes, by silken fringes veiled,
Clouds darkly shading their celestial blue,
That melt in dewy sadness if he hears
Some moving tales, how "once two hapless babes
Were left alone to perish in a wood,
And there in one another's arms they died,
And Robin Redbreast covered them with leaves"—
That gentle child must be a man of peace—
He cannot brave the buffets of the world;
And yet, with all his meekness—who can tell?—
The boy may live to be a bishop yet.
And little Annie—what will Annie be?
The fair-haired prattler! she, with matron airs,
Who gravely lectures her rebellious doll—
"Annie will be papa's own darling child,
Dear papa's blessing." Ah, she tells thee truth!—
The pretty mockbird with his borrowed notes
Tells thee sweet truth! Already, is she not
Thy darling child? Thy blessing she will prove,
The duteous prop of thy declining years.
Thy sons will rove, as various fortune leads,
Haply successful in their several paths,
And, like thyself, in course of years, become
The careful fathers of a hopeful race;
Then will ambitious thoughts and worldly cares
Engross their hearts, and haply steal from thee
A portion of thy former influence then—
But *she* will never change. That tender heart,
Though wedded love and infant claimants dear

May waken there new interests—new and sweet—
Thine in that loving heart will ne'er decrease;
'Tis rich in kind affections, and can give—
Ay, largely give—without despoiling thee:
Thou wilt partake her ever watchful cares;
Her husband, for her sake, will cherish thee;
Her children will be taught to honour thee;
And while they fondly swarm about thy chair,
Or climb thy knees, th' endearing witchery
Will half renew again *her* infant days.
It is not love that steals the heart from love;
'Tis the hard world, and its perplexing cares;
Its petrifying selfishness, its pride,
Its low ambition, and its paltry aims.

Those happy evenings! ay, 'twas there I left—
The landscape finished, young invention sought,
Not often baffled, springs of fresh delight,
And found them frequent, Goldsmith, in thy work
Of 'Animated Nature'—precious book!
Illustrated with pictures, that to me
Rivalled at least the subjects they adorned;
Then with sharp scissors armed—a jealous loan
With many a solemn charge conceded slow—
And fair unwrinkled paper, soon began
The imitative labour: and anon
Wide o'er the table ranged a motley herd,
A heterogeneous multitude, before
Never assembled thus, since that old time
When Noah to the finished ark called in
Of every species the allotted pair.
There first the unwieldy elephant advanced,
Majestic beast! on whose stupendous bulk
Raja or Sultan might have sat sublime;

The Birthday. 15

Next in the line of march, ill-mated pair!
With branching antlers and slight flexile limbs,
Comes on the graceful dweller of the north;
He whose winged swiftness, like an arrow's flight,
Wafts the rude sledge, that bears o'er Lapland snows
The stinted native of those cheerless plains.
The Arab's faithful servant follows next,
The patient camel, useful to the last—
Who, when he sinks upon the burning sand
Beneath his burthen, slakes his master's thirst,
Slain for its sake, with the long-hoarded draught.
Then came the warrior bison, strong ally
Of his rude lord, grim guardian of his herds,
And sharer of his cabin comforts few.

Thus had I learnt of each brief history
From those illumined pages, to relate,
Too oft, I fear, to undelighted ears,
When with triumphant pleasure I displayed
The wonders of that paper menagerie—
But not as then will I enumerate now,
From the grim lion to the timorous hare,
Each by his several title, name, and style —
Or notice, but with glancing mention brief,
Those higher aims of art, creating shapes—
Not likenesses of aught in heaven or earth—
That with self-gratulating pride I called
Orlando and Rogero—names renowned!
And Bradamant, and fair Angelica—
For I had read with eager interest,
Half comprehending, that romantic tale.
And thine immortal Epic, sightless Bard!
In Pope's smooth verse revealed to ears unlearned,
Supplied a subject that, recalled, e'en now

Provokes me to a smile; so strange the choice;
That novel illustration so uncouth.
'Twas when forth issuing from the Cyclops' cave
The wily Ithacan Ulysses came,
Locked in the shaggy fleeces of the ram,
Behind his Centaur flock. Incongruous pairs!
Biped and quadruped together linked.
Ulysses never bound his trembling crew
More carefully beneath the guardian's fleece
Than I secured their paper effigies
To sheep, for height and bulk, proportions huge!
Worthy, indeed, to be a giant's flock.

How vivid still, how deep the hues, the imprint
Left by those childish pastimes! Later joys,
Less puerile, more exciting have I known—
Ah! purer none; from earth's alloy so free—
But Memory hoards no picture so distinct,
In freshness as of yesterday, as those
Life's first impressions, exquisite and strong—
Their stamp, compared to that of later days,
Like a proof print from the engraver's plate,
The first struck off—most forcibly imprest.
Lo! what a train like Bluebeard's wives appear,
So many headless, half dismembered some,
With battered faces—eyeless—noseless—grim
With cracked enamel, and unsightly scars—
Some with bald pates, or hempen wigs unfrizzed,
And ghastly stumps, like Greenwich pensioners;
Others mere Torsos—arms, legs, heads, all gone!
But precious all. And chief that veteran doll,
She from whose venerable face is worn
All prominence of feature; shining brown,
Like chestnut from its prickly coating freed,

The Birthday.

With equal polish as the wigless skull—
Well I remember, with what bribery won
Of a fair rival—one of waxen mould—
Long coveted possession!—I was brought
The mutilated favourite to resign.
The blue-eyed fair one came—perfection's self!
With eager joy I clasped her waxen charms;
But then—the stipulated sacrifice!
"And must we part?" my piteous looks expressed—
Mute eloquence! "And *must* we part, dear Stump!"
"Oh! might I keep ye both!"—and both I kept.

Unwelcome hour, I ween, that tied me down
Restless, reluctant, to the sempstress' task!
Sight horrible to me, th' allotted seam
Of stubborn Irish, or more hateful length
Of handkerchief, with folded edge tacked down,
All to be hemmed; ay, *selvidge sides* and all.
And so they were in tedious course of time,
With stitches long and short, "cat's teeth" yclept;
Or jumbled thick and thin, oblique, transverse,
At last, in sable line imprinted grim.
But less distasteful was the sampler's task;
There green and scarlet vied; and fancy claimed
Her privilege to crowd the canvass field
With hearts and zigzags, strawberries and leaves,
And many a quaint device; some moral verse,
Or Scripture text, enwrought; and, last of all,
Last, though not least, the self-pleased artist's name.

And yet, with more alacrity of will,
I fashioned various raiment; caps, cloaks, gowns;
Gay garments for the family of dolls;
No matter how they fitted—they were *made;*

Ay, and applauded, and rewarded too
With silver thimble. Precious gift! bestowed
By a kind aunt; one ever kind and good,
Mine early benefactress! Since approved
By time and trial mine unchanging friend;
Yet most endeared by the affecting bond
Of mutual sorrows, mutual sympathies.

Yet was that implement, the first possessed,
Proudly possessed, indeed, but seldom worn.
Easier to me, and pleasanter, to poke,
As one should poke a skewer, the needle through
With thumb and finger, than in silver thrall
To imprison the small tip, too tiny still
For smallest thimble ever made to fit.
Dear aunt! you should have sought in wizard lore
The name of some artificer, empowered
By royal patent of the Elfin Court
To make Mab's thimble—if the sprightly Queen
Ever indeed vouchsafes in regal sport,
With needle, from the eyelash of a fly,
Plucked sharp and shining, and fine cobweb-thread,
To embroider her light scarf of gossamer.
Not oft, I doubt; she better loves to rove
Where trembling harebells on the green hillside
Wave in their azure beauty; or to slide
On a slant sunbeam down the fragrant tube
Of honeysuckle or sweet columbine,
And sip luxurious the ambrosial feast
Stored there for nature's alchymist, the bee;
Then satiate, and at rest, to sleep secure,
Even in that perfumed chamber, till the sun
Has ploughed with flaming wheels the Atlantic wave,
And the dark beetle, her mailed sentinel,

The Birthday.

Winds his shrill signal to invite her forth.
Not on her waking hour such pomp attends,
As when on Ohio's banks magnolias tall
Embalm the dews of night, and living sparks
Glance through the leaves, and star the deep serene.
But even here, in our romantic isle,
The pearl of ocean, girdled with its foam!
Land of the rainbow! even here she loves
The dewy freshness of the silent hour,
Whose gentle waftings have their incense too,
To scatter in her paths; the faint perfume
Of dog-rose pale, or aromatic breath
Of purple wild thyme, clouding the green sward;
And though in air no sparkling myriads dart
Their glancing fires to light the Fairy Queen,
Earth hath her stars, a living emerald each!
And by the lustre of those dewy gems
She trips it deftly with her merry train
In mossy dells, around the time-scarred trunk
Of giant oak, or neath the wych-elm's shade,
Beside some deep dark pool, where one bright star
Trembles reflected, or in velvet meads,
Where, though the limpid blade of tender grass
Bends not beneath the "many-twinkling" feet,
Dark circles on the paler sward defined
Reveal at morning where the dance has been;
Oft thickly studded with a mushroom belt,
The fungus growth of one short summer's night,
The ring so geometrically drawn,
As if the gnomes, with scientific skill,
Forming the fairy sports, had mimicked there
The circling rampart of a Celtic camp,
Or with more apt similitude designed
The Druid's holy ring of pale-grey stones.

There oft the milkmaid, when with shining pail
She seeks the glistening pasture, finds dispersed
The relics of the banquet, leaves and flowers,
From golden kingcups cropped, and poplars white,
The cups and trenchers of the midnight feast.
Ah, lucky lass! when stirring with the lark,
On dairy charge intent, she thither hies,
And finds her task forestalled—the cool tiled floor
Flooded, fresh sluiced—stool, shelf, and slab bright rubbed—
Scalded and sweet the glazy milk-pans all,
And scoured to silver sheen the ready pail,
And, brighter still, within its circle left,
The glittering sixpence—industry's reward.

Me more delighted in the fairy's haunts
To sport, like them an airy gleesome sprite,
Than, prisoner of an hour—e'en that too long—
The needle's task monotonous to ply.
But I have lived to prize the humble art—
To number with the happiest of my life
Those quiet evenings, when with busy hands
I plied the needle, listening as I wrought—
By that mechanical employ, more fixed
Attention apt to rove—to that dear voice
Which from some favourite author read aloud.
The voice is silent, and the task laid by—
Distasteful now, when silence, with a tongue
More audibly intelligent than speech
For ever whispers round me, "She is gone."

A day to be remembered well was that,
When, by my father taught, I first essayed
The early rudiments of penmanship.
Long-wished-for lesson! by prudential love—

The Birthday.

Wisely considerate of my infant years—
Withheld, till granted slow in fair exchange
For some relinquished pleasure; 'twas received
A twofold grant—a boon and a reward.
So I began, long rigorously confined
To rows of sloping strokes. Not *sloping* all;
At first in straggling piles they jostled rude,
Like raw recruits, till into order drilled,
Maintaining equal distance on their march,
Even and close they ranged like veteran troops,
In ranks symmetrical; and *then* at last
My long restrained ambition was indulged
In higher flights, with nicer art to shape
The involutions of the alphabet.
Unsteady and perplexed the first attempts—
Great A's, that with colossal strides encroached
On twice the space they should have occupied,
And I's like T's, and R's whose lower limbs
Beyond the upper bulged unseemly out,
And sprawling W's, and V's, and Y's,
Gaping prodigiously, like butter-boats.
But soon succeeded to those shapeless scrawls
Fair capitals and neat round characters,
Erelong in words and sentences combined;
At first restrained between two guiding lines,
Then ranged on one—that one continued long,
Spite of ambitious daring, that would fain
Have strayed, from limit and restriction free;
For ardently I longed to scrawl at will
The teeming fancies of a busy brain,
Not half content, not satisfied, albeit
My father, with a kind and ready pen,
Vouchsafed assistance to the infant muse.

* * * * * *

The Birthday.

Smile, gentle reader—if so be, in sooth,
Reader shall e'er these simple records scan,—
But not in mockery of supposed conceit
Proud of precocious genius. I too smile
In sad humility, experience-taught,
At thought of the young daring, by fond hearts
Built on exultingly. Alas, dear friends!
No heaven-born genius, as ye simply deemed,
Stirred in my childish heart the love of song;
'Twas feeling, finely organised perhaps
To keen perceptions of the beautiful,
The great in art or nature, sight or sound,
The working of a restless spirit, long
For every pastime cast upon itself—
I was an only child, and never knew
The social pleasures of a schoolgirl's life.
All these, with other circumstance combined,
As those first lessons from the books I named,
And rural occupations, tuned my soul
Aye, every trembling chord, to poesie.
Books were my playfellows, and trees and flowers,
And murmuring rivulets, and merry birds,
And painted insects, all were books to me,
And breathed a language, from the dawn of sense
Familiar to my heart: what marvel, then,
If, like an echo, wakened by the tone
Of Nature's music, faint response I made?
And so I stood beside my father's knee,
Dictating, while he wrote, wild rhapsodies
Of "vales and hills enamelled o'er with flowers,
Like those of Eden, white with fleecy flocks"—
Of "silver streams, by spring's warm breath unbound,
And winter past and gone."

The Birthday.

       Most simple themes,
Set to a few low notes monotonous,
Like the first chirping of a nestling bird,
Quavering uncertain! But parental hearts
Hailed them as heavenly music, to their ear
Prelusive of rich volumed harmonies.
Fond hopes! illusive as the march-fire's light;
Yet, *not* like that, in utter darkness quenched.
Nature in me hath still her worshipper,
And in my soul her mighty spirit still
Awakes sweet music, tones, and symphonies,
Struck by the master-hand from every chord.
But prodigal of feeling, she withholds
The glorious power to pour its fulness out;
And in mid-song I falter, faint at heart,
With consciousness that every feeble note
But yields to the awakening harmony
A weak response—a trembling echo still.

Revive, dear healthful pastimes! active sports
Of childhood's enterprising age, revive!
Elastic aye! untiring, unsubdued
By labour, disappointment, or fatigue:
Thy toil enjoyment—thy defeated hope
The spur to fresh exertion—thy fatigue
The healthful anodyne that medicines thee
To renovating slumbers light and sweet.
Full oft I pause with reminiscent eye
Upon the little spot of border-ground
Once called "*my* garden." Proud accession that
To territorial right and power supreme!
To *right possessive*, the exclusive *mine*,
So soon asserted, e'en by infant tongue.
Methinks the thick-sown parallels I see

Of thriving mustard—herb of rapid growth!
The only one whose magical increase
Keeps pace with young impatience, that expects
Ripe pulse to-morrow from seed sown to-day.
To-morrow and to-morrow passes on,
And still no vestige of the incipient plant.
No longer to be borne, the third day's sun
Beholds the little fingers delving deep
T' unearth the buried seed; and up it comes,
Just swelling into vegetable life;
Of which assured, into the mould again
'Tis stuck, *a little nearer to the top.*
Such was the process horticultural
I boldly practised in my new domain:
As little chance of rest, as little chance
To live and thrive, had slip or cutting there,
Which failing in three days to sprout amain,
Was twitched impatient up, with curious eye
Examined, and if fibrous threads appeared,
With renovated hope replanted soon.

But thriving plants *were* there, though not of price.
No puny children of a foreign soil,
But hardy natives of our own dear earth,
From many a field and bank and streamlet side
Transplanted careful, with the adhering mould.
The primrose, with her large indented leaves
And many blossoms pale, expanded there,
With wild anemone, and hyacinth,
And languid cowslip, lady of the mead,
And violets' mingled hues of every sort,
Blue, white, and purple. The more fragrant white
Even from that very root, in many a patch
Extended wide, still scents the garden round.

The Birthday.

Maternal love received the childish gift,
A welcome offering, and the lowly flower,
A rustic stranger, bloomed with cultured sweets;
And still it shares their bed, encroaching oft—
So ignorance presumes—on worthier claims.
She spared it in the tenderness of love,
Her child's first gift; and I, for her dear sake,
Who prized the pale intruder, spare it now.

Loved occupations! blameless, calm delights!
Your relish has not palled upon my sense;
I taste ye with as keen enjoyment still
As in my childish days; with zeal as warm,
More temperate, less impatient, still I tend
My flowery charge, with interest unimpaired
Watching the tender germ and swelling bud,
Pruning the weak or too luxuriant shoot,
And timely propping with assiduous care
The slender stalks with heavy blossoms bowed.
I will not tell how lately and how oft
In dreams I've wandered 'mongst the blooming tribes,
Continuing thus in sleep the pleasing task,
My summer evening's toil. I will not tell
How lately, stealing forth on moonless night,
I've sought by lantern light the dewy buds
Of peeping larkspur, searching 'mong the leaves
For nightly spoilers, from the soft light earth
That issue forth to feed on the young plant,
Their favourite dainty. No, I will not tell,
Lest wisdom laugh to scorn such puerile cares
In age mature, how lately they've been mine.
The gladness! the unspeakable deep joy!
When Nature, putting off her russet stole
Of wintry sadness, decks herself afresh

In bloom and beauty, like a virgin bride.
With lovely coyness, shrinkingly she comes;
For oft in clouds, and mist, and arrowy sleet,
The sun, her bridegroom, veils his glorious face,
And on his setting hour too often hangs
The breath of lingering frosts, repelling long
All but the hardiest children of the spring.
Of these, the earliest pursuivants, appear,
Studding the brown earth with their golden stars,
The clustering aconites, a pigmy race,
Fearless of wintry blast, whose fiercest rage
Passes innocuous o'er their lowly bed.
But soon through every border the moist earth
Breaks up its even surface, every clod
Expands and heaves with vegetable life;
And tender cones of palest green appear,
The future hyacinths, and arrowy points
Of bolder crocus; and the bashful heads
Of snowdrops, trembling on their slender stalks;
And next, of many hues, hepaticas,
The red, the milk-white, and the lovelier blue—
A vegetable amethyst!—come forth,
The impatient blossoms bursting into sight
Before the tardier leaves; but those at length
Expand their outward circle, fencing round
With its broad fringe the tufted bloom within.
But Winter oft, tenacious of his sway,
Enviously lingers on the skirts of Spring,
Binds up in frozen chains the stubborn soil,
Nips the young leaf, and checks the tender germ.
In such ungenial seasons oft I've watched
Week after week, and shivered at the sight,
Beneath some shelving bank or garden wall
Long wreaths of snow, that on the border mould,

The Birthday.

In drifted thickness heaped, continuous lie.
Elsewhere divested of that livery pale,
The cold Earth reassumes her natural hues,
And slow returning verdure: but in vain
To the stiff surface heave the tender heads
Of budding flowers, or if they struggle through,
Deep in their sheltering leaves concealed they lie.

At length succeeds a thaw—a rapid thaw;
And from the heavens a dazzling sun looks down,
Arousing Nature from her torpid thrall.
Yielding and moist becomes the darkening mould.
And from that snow-heaped border melts away
The drifted wreath ;—it shrinks and disappears,
And lo! as by enchantment, in its place
A rainbow streaks the ground—a flowery prism
Of crocus tribes innumerous, to the Sun
Expanding wide their gold and purple stars.

A Christian moral—to the pious mind
All things present one—may be found e'en here.
Adversity, like that pale wreath of snow,
Falls on the youthful heart, a seeming load
Of deadly pressure, crushing its young hopes;
But *seeming* such, for after certain space
Continuing there, and if it finds the soil
Not wholly sterile, to the frozen mass
Of its own latent virtues it imparts
A fertilising warmth, that penetrates
The surface of obdurate worldliness.
Then from the barren waste, no longer such,
Upspring a thousand amaranthine flowers
"Whose fragrance smells to heaven." Desires chastised,

Enlarged affections, tender charities,
Long-suffering mercy, and the snowdrop buds
Of heavenly meekness :—These, and thousands more
As beautiful, as kindly, are called forth,
Adversity! beneath thy fostering shade.

PART THE SECOND.

CONTENTS.

The Willow-tree.—The Swing.—The Old Parrot.—The Toad.—The Mechanic.—My Spaniel.—Juba.—Birds and Beasts.—Humanity.—Sensibility.—Sportsmen.—My Hare.—Old Ephraim.—Travelled Puppies.—Sympathy.—Conoscenti.

HARD by that flourishing domain, that strip
Of border ground, my garden, late described,
On a grass plot by the house door there stood
An aged willow, whose long flexile boughs
With their light shadows checkered the green turf;
Beneath the sheltering arms of that old tree
Pastime, to me delightful, oft I found
On balanced seat, upborne by a strong limb
Selected for the trust with cautious care,
Anxious as his, who for an arctic voyage
Of unknown peril, far discovery,
Selects the timbers for some strong-ribbed bark :
Even with like caution did my father choose
The transverse bough to which his hands made fast
With firmness doubly sure the swinging cords;
Committing to their strength a freight to him
More precious, than to Solomon of old
The yearly lading of his treasure-ships

The Birthday.

From Tarshish and from Ophir—ay, than those
To the great Hebrew—than the wealth of worlds—!
Far, far more precious to my father's heart
That bending bough's light weight—his only child.

Right pleasant pastime! the clear cutting air
To cleave with rapid motion, self-impelled—
For I was dexterous at the sport—to sway
With pendulous slow motion, dying off
To scarce perceptible, until at last
Settling to perfect stillness; which, howe'er,
A breath, a finger's motion would disturb.
So 'twas my luxury to sit and dream,
Building in cloud-land many a castle fair,
Albeit no genii of the ring or lamp
Came at my bidding; in those dreamy moods
I conjured up as gorgeous palaces—
Gardens as dazzling bright with jewelled fruit
As e'er Aladdin's wondering eyes beheld,
And peopled them with living forms, to me,
Deep read in magic lore, familiar all.
Then the Commander of the Faithful strayed,
And dark Mesrour, and that devoted slave
Giafar, the pearl of ministers, whose head
So lightly on his patient shoulders sat,
Ready to leave them headless, at a nod
From his most gracious master. Stately walked
Beside her mighty lord his jealous spouse,
Scornful Zobeide, their attendant slaves
Close following; the fair Noushatoul; and he
The Caliph's favourite, jester of the court,
Facetious Abon Hassan. Hunchback, too,
And that loquacious Barber, and his train
Of luckless brethren, came at my command.

Then, with King Saladin and Queen Gulnare,
A car of pearl and coral bore me off
Through submarine dominions—overarched
With liquid chrysolite the billowy vault;
Or with the exiled brethren far I strayed,
Amgrad and Assad, or that happier prince
Who found the hall of statues, found and won
That ninth, so far surpassing all the rest.

Anon I ventured on a darker realm,
Peopled with awful shapes—magicians dire,
Happak and Ulin, and their hideous crew,
The Sultan Misnar's leagued inveterate foes.
How my heart beat, as in the dead of night
With him and his suspected slave I trod
Those rocky passages, hewn roughly out
In the earth's entrails! How I held my breath,
Expecting the result, when through the ring
The severed rope slid rapidly away!
How my young feelings sympathised with hers,
The duteous Una's, when on Tigris' banks,
A weeping orphan, she was left forlorn;
And when in urgent peril—hapless maid!
In that dark forest from her side she missed
The guardian peppercorns! But oh! the joy
When in the shaggy monarch of the woods,
A brave protector—brave and kind—she found.
I saw her by his side—in his thick mane
I saw her small white fingers fondly twined;
Majestically gentle, at her feet
I saw the royal brute lie fawning down;
I saw all this—and murmured half aloud,
"Oh how I wish I had a lion too!"

The Birthday.

Fantastic shadows! fearful, gay, grotesque!
Still with a child's delight I reperuse
The pages where ye live; recall ye still—
Ay, all your marvellous annals—with as keen
And undiminished interest as of yore
When I convened ye at my sovereign will
In that green bower beneath the willow-tree,
Where moments flew uncounted as I sat
With eyes half-closed, excluding outward things;
And as the spell within worked languidly,
Or kindled into action, truth, and life,
Slower or faster swung my airy car—
Not *quite* at rest, for that had broke the charm—
Unconscious I so tranced in waking dreams,
That mine own impulse checked or urged it on.

But I was not sole tenant of the tree,
Not then companionless: above my head
Among the thicker branches, there secure
From the swing's reach, our old grey parrot hung—
Poor Poll! we were in truth well-sorted mates.
Wert thou my prototype? or I in sooth
The shadow of thy graces and thy wit?
As Jacko in the fable proveth plain
That man, the servile copyist! apes his.
Associates though we were in that green bower,
Yet little kindness, Poll! betwixt us grew;
For many an ancient grudge in either heart
Kept us asunder, and the hag Mistrust
Widened the unhealed wounds of former feuds.
Thou wert, in truth, the aggressor in those feuds,
For, Poll! it ill became thy reverend years,
With spiteful vengeance of that hard sharp beak
The unsuspecting freedom to repulse

The Birthday.

Of baby fondness, first encouraged, too,
By coaxing treachery—"Scratch poor Polly's head."
And when thy victim, smarting with the pain
Of that unkind reception, wept aloud,
'Twas most ungenerous, Poll! to flout and jeer,
And mock with imitative whine, and cry,
And peevish whimper, and convulsive sob,
Concluding all with boisterous ha! ha! ha!

Then comments indiscreet of mutual friends—
Such oftenest the result—but served to increase
And whet the growing animosity.
The frowning hearer, when I gabbled o'er
Some tedious lesson, not a word whereof
Informed my far-off senses, bade me note
How Poll as glibly ran *her* lesson o'er
Of words by her as little understood.
The mincing nursemaid, sedulous to improve
The graces of her charge, reproached me oft
With turned-in toes—"for all the world like Poll."
And when my heart with rage rebellious swelled—
Alas! 'twas a rebellious little heart—
And angrily I stamped the tiny foot,
And screamed aloud, the bird screamed louder still;
And I was told to mark how even Poll
Despised and laughed to shame the naughty girl.

As babyhood's first lisping years wore on,
Monitions such as these their influence lost,
And to the noisy mimic's flout and jeer
A careless callous listener I became;
But distance due was still between us kept
With strict punctilio—an armed, neutral peace,
Never infringed by familiarity.

The Birthday.

So there together in the willow-tree
Our several pastimes Poll and I pursued;
Some much resembling still, for to and fro,
Exalted in her wiry globe, she swung,
As if to mimic there my sport below.

Thou wert the only creature, bird or beast,
Excluded from my lavish fondness, Poll!
Fowls of the air, and beasts, and creeping things,
Ay, reptiles—slimy creatures—all that breathed
The breath of life, found favour in my sight;
And strange disgust I've seen (*I* thought it strange)
Wrinkle their features who beheld me touch,
Handle, caress the creatures they abhorred;
Enchase my finger with the palmer-worm
Or caterpillar's green, cold, clammy ring,
Or touch the rough back of the spotted toad.
One of that species, for long after years,
Even till of late, became my pensioner—
A monstrous creature!—It was wont to sit
Among the roots of an old scraggy shrub,
A huge Gum-Cystus: All the summer long
" Princess Hemjunah "—titled so by me
In honour of that royal spell-bound fair
So long compelled in reptile state to crawl—
" Princess Hemjunah " there, from morn to eve,
Made her pavilion of the spicy shrub;
And they who looked beneath it scarce discerned
That living clod from the surrounding mould,
But by the lustre of two living gems
That from the reptile's forehead upward beamed
Intelligent, with ever-wakeful gaze.
There daily on some fresh green leaf I spread
A luscious banquet for that uncouth guest—

C

Milk, cream, and sugar,—to the creature's taste
Right welcome offering, unrejected still.

When autumn winds 'gan strew the crispèd leaves
Round that old Cystus, to some lonelier haunt,
Some dark retreat, the hermit Reptile crawled:
Belike some grotto, 'neath the hollow roots
Of ancient laurel or thick juniper,
Whose everlasting foliage darkly gleamed
Through the bare branches of deciduous trees.
There, self-immured the livelong winter through,
Brooded unseen the solitary thing:
E'en when young Spring with violet-printed steps
Brushed the white hoar-frost from her morning path,
The creature stirred not from its secret cell:
But on some balmy morn of ripening June,
Some morn of perfect summer, wakened up
With choirs of music poured from every bush,
Dews dropping incense from the unfolding leaves
Of half-blown roses, and the gentle South
Exhaling, blending, and diffusing sweets—
Then was I sure on some such morn to find
My Princess crouched in her accustomed form
Beneath the Cystus.   So for many years—
Ay, as I said, till late, she came and went,
And came again when summer suns returned—
All knew and spared the creature for my sake,
Not without comment on the strange caprice
Protecting such deformed, detested thing.
But in a luckless hour—an autumn morn,
About the time when my poor Toad withdrew,
Annually punctual, to her winter house—
The axe and pruning-knife were set at work;—

The Birthday.

Ah, uncle Philip! with unsparing zeal
You urged them on, to lop the straggling boughs
Whose rank luxuriance from the parent stem
Drained for their useless growth too large supply;
Branch after branch condemned fell thickly round,
Till, moderate reform intended first—
Nice task to fix the boundary!—edged on,
Encroaching still to radical; and soon
Unchecked the devastating fury raged,
And shoots, and boughs, and limbs bestrewed the ground,
And all denuded and exposed—sad sight!
The mangled trees held out their ghastly stumps.

Spring reappeared, and trees and shrubs put forth
Their budding leaves, and e'en those mangled trunks,
Though later, felt the vegetable life
Mount in their swelling sap, and all around
The recently dismembered parts, peeped out
Pink tender shoots disparting into green,
And bursting forth at last, with rapid growth,
In full redundance, healthful, vigorous, thick;
And June returned with all her breathing sweets,
Her opening roses and soft southern gales;
And music poured from every bending spray;
E'en the old mangled Cystus bloomed once more,
But my poor Princess never came again.

More beauteous graceful pensioners were those—
But not more harmless—on the gravel walk
Before our parlour-window, from my hand
That pecked their daily dole of scattered crumbs.
Welcome and safe was each confiding guest,
Though favour with a partial hand strewed thick

The crumbled shower in Robin Redbreast's way;
But all were welcome,—Blackbirds, Thrushes,
    Wrens,
Finches, and chirping Sparrows.
                              How I hate
Those London Sparrows! Vile, pert, noisy things!
Whose ceaseless clamour at the window-sill—
The back-room window opening on some mews—
Reminds one of the country just so far
As to bemock its wild and blithesome sounds,
And press upon the heart our pent-up state
In the great Babylon;—oppressed, engulfed
By crowds, and smoke, and vapour: where one sees,
For laughing vales fair winding in the sun,
And hill-tops gleaming in his golden light,
The dingy red of roofs and chimneys tall
On which a leaden orb looks dimly down!
For limpid rills, the kennel's stream impure;
For primrose banks, the rifled, scentless things
Tied up for sale, held out by venal hands;
For lowing herds and bleating flocks, the cries
Of noisy venders threading every key
From bass to treble, of discordant sound;
For trees, unnatural stinted mockeries
At windows, and on balconies stuck up
Fir-trees in vases!—picturesque conceit!—
Whereon, to represent the woodland choir,
Perch those sweet songsters of the sooty wing.

  * * * * * *

Yet, as I write, the light and flippant mood
Changes to one of serious saddened thought,
And my heart smites me for the sorry jest,
Calling to mind a sight that filled me once
With tenderest sympathy.

The Birthday.

In a great city,
Blackened and deafening with the smoke and din
Of forge and engine, Traffic's thriving mart,
Chartered by Mammon, underneath a range
Of gorgeous show-rooms, where all precious metals,
In forms innumerous, exquisitely wrought,
Dazzled the gazer's eye, I visited
The secret places of the "Prison House."
From den to den of a long file I passed
Of dingy workshops, each affording space
But for the sallow inmate and his tools:
His table, the broad, timeworn, blackened slab
Of a deep sunken window, whose dim panes
Tinged with a sickly hue the blessed beams
Of the bright noonday sun. I tarried long
In one of those sad cells, conversing free
With its pale occupant, a dark-browed man,
Of hard, repellant aspect, hard and stern.
But having watched awhile the curious sleight
Of his fine handicraft, when I expressed
Pleased admiration, in few words, but frank,
And toned by kindly feeling—for my heart
Yearned with deep sympathy—the moody man
Looked up into my face, and in that look
Flashed out an intellectual soul-fraught gleam
Of pleased surprise, that changed to mild and good
The harsh expression of that care-marred face.
There lay beside him on the window slab
A dirty ragged book turned downwards open
Where he had last been reading, from his toil
Snatching a hurried moment. Anxiously
I glanced towards it, but forbore to question,
Restrained by scrupulous feeling, shunning most
Shadow of disrespect to low estate;

But from the book my wandering gaze passed on
To where, beyond it, close to the dim panes,
A broken flower-pot, with a string secured,
Contained a living treasure—a green clump,
Just bursting into bloom, of the field orchis.
"You care for flowers," I said; "and that fair
  thing,
The beautiful orchis, seems to flourish well
With little light and air."
 "It won't for long,"
The man made answer, with a mournful smile
Eyeing the plant—" I took it up, poor thing!
But Sunday evening last from the rich meadow
Where thousands bloom so gay, and brought it here
To smell of the green fields for a few days
Till Sunday comes again, and rest mine eyes on
When I look up fatigued from these dead gems
And yellow glittering gold."
 With patient courtesy,
Well spoken, clear (no ignorant churl was he),
That poor artificer explained the process
Of his ingenious art. I looked and listened,
But with an aching heart, that loathed the sight
Of those bright pebbles and that glittering ore;
And when I turned to go—not unexpressed
My feelings of goodwill and thankfulness—
He put into my hand a small square packet
Containing powder, that would quite restore,
He told me, to dull gems and clouded pearls
Their pristine lustre. I received, well pleased,
Proffering payment; but he shook his head,
Motioning back my hand, and stooping down
Resumed his task, in a low, deep-toned voice
Saying, "You're kindly welcome."

The Birthday.

                    Gems and pearls
Abound not in my treasury, but there
I hoard with precious things the poor man's gift.

But what have I to do—distasteful theme!—
With towns and cities? Thither unawares
Wild fancy wandered, but, recalled as soon,
Wings back her way, and lights at home once more—
Lights down amid the furred and feathered court
That owned my sovereign sway—a motley train!
Rabbits and birds, and dormice, cats and kittens,
And dogs of many a race, from ancient Di,
My father's faithful setter, to black Mungo
And mine own favourite spaniel—*most mine own*.

My poor old Chloe! gentle playfellow!
Most patient, most enduring was thy love;
To restless childhood's teasing fondness proof,
And its tormenting ingenuity.
Methinks I see thee in some corner stuck,
In most unnatural posture, bolt upright,
With rueful looks and drooping ears forlorn,
Thy two fore-paws, to hold my father's cane—
Converted to a musket—cramped across.
Then wert thou posted like a sentinel
Till numbers ten were slowly counted o'er—
That welcome tenth! the signal sound to thee
Of penance done and liberty regained!
Down went the cane, and from thy corner forth,
With uproar wild and madly frolic joy,
Bounding aloft, and wheeling round and round
With mirth-inviting antics, didst thou spring.
And the grave teacher—grave no longer—shared
The boisterous pupil's loud unbridled glee.

Then were there dismal outcries, shrill complaints,
From angry Jane, of frocks and petticoats
All grim with muddy stains and ghastly rents.
"'Twas all in vain," the indignant damsel vowed—
"'Twas all in vain to toil for such a child—
For such a Tom-boy! Climbing up great trees—
Scrambling through brake and bush, and hedge and
    ditch,
For paltry wild-flowers. Always without gloves,
Grubbing the earth up like a little pig
With her own nails, and, just as bad as *he*,
Racing and romping with that dirty beast."
Then followed serious—"But the time will come
You'll be ashamed, Miss, of such vulgar ways:
You a young lady!—Not much like one now."
Too oft unmoved by the pathetic zeal
Of such remonstrance, pertly I replied,
"No, Mistress Jane! that time will never come.
When I'm grown up I'll romp with Chloe still,
As I do now; and climb and scramble too
After sweet wild-flowers just as much as now;
And 'grub the earth,' and 'never put on gloves.'
Then if I dirt my hands and tear my frock,
You'll not dare scold when I'm a woman grown;
For who would mind your scolding, Mistress Jane?"

Alas, poor maid! an arduous task was thine—
A hopeless, labour, recommencing still,
Like theirs, the unhappy sisters, doomed to pour
Eternal streams in jars that never fill.

Next in degree to the old faithful dog,
Next in my favouring fondness, Juba ranked.
Sprung of a race renowned, in Juba's veins

The Birthday.

The mettled blood of noble coursers ran.
Foaled on my father's land, his sprightly youth
Sported, like mine, those pleasant meads among,
And when I saw him first, a new-born thing,
Tottering and trembling by the old mare's side
On his long slender limbs, I called him then,
And thenceforth he was called, "My little horse."
And soon those slender, flexile limbs were braced
With sinewy strength, and soon that feeble frame
Expanded into vigorous, noble bulk;
From his broad swelling chest arched proudly up,
With graceful curve, the yet unbridled neck;
Free to the winds, the flowing mane and tail
In their wild beauty streamed exuberant out,
Or lashed the glossy chestnut of his sides
With dark dishevelled flakes; and his small ears,
With flexile beauty oft inverting quick
Their black-fringed edges; and those large bright eyes,
Flashing with all the fire of youth and joy,
And freedom uncontrolled! I see him now,
My gallant Juba! racing round the field,
Fleet as the whirlwind, with down-arching neck,
Yet stately in its bend, and clattering hoofs,
And long back-streaming tail. In mid career,
Self-checked and suddenly, he stops abrupt,
Back on his haunches gathering proudly up
His bulk majestic, and with head flung back
Disdainfully aside, and eyes of flame,
And nostrils wide distended, firmly forth
He straightens one black, sinewy, slender limb,
The other, gathered inward, touches scarce
The ground with its bent hoof. Then loud and clear
Echoes o'er hill and dale his long shrill neigh,

And e'er the sound expires, with snort and stamp
Away he starts, and scours the field again.
But oft at sight of me—full well he knew
His fairy mistress—oft at sight of me,
With whinnying welcome, and familiar eye,
Yet shyly curious, he came trotting up
Expectant, the accustomed feast to claim,
Apple or crust, that I was wont to bring.

I have not specified the creatures half,
My sometime favourites. Should I notice each,
Paper would fail, and patience be worn out
Of most indulgent reader. Such a throng!
Jackdaws and magpies, turtle-doves and owls,
And squirrels, playful in captivity,
But still untamed. Most barbarous to immure
The pretty sylvan in a small close cage;
Painful to watch the everlasting round
The restless prisoner circles all day long
Monotonous—sad mockery of mirth!—
Within his narrow limits. Wretched change
From the wild haunts, where erst, from tree to tree
He leaped and gambolled all the summer long,
The very life of liberty and joy.
Mine was an old maimed creature, maimed for life
By the vile treacherous snare, and happier since—
So I concluded—in its captive state
Of plenteous ease, than helplessly at large
Among its hardier fellows of the woods.
A very hospital, in truth, I kept
For such dumb patients, maimed, diseased, and old.
The squirrel just described, a veteran then,
Had just precedence; next in age and rank
Hopped an old bulfinch, of one leg bereft,

The Birthday.

By what untoward accident the bird
Brought no certificate. A sportsman once—
None of the keenest—brought me bleeding home
A wounded leveret, not quite hurt to death,
But sorely mangled. From its mother's side
Scarce could the little creature yet have strayed,
When all too well that fatal shot was aimed.
Perhaps that luckless morning was the first
Among the dewy herbs and tender grass
That the poor mother led her young one forth
To taste the sweets of life—that sacred gift
Of its Almighty Maker. Was the boon
Bestowed to be abused in cruel sport
By Man, into whose nostrils the same power
Breathed with creating will the breath of life?
I know for Man's convenience and support,
Nay, for his luxuries, the inferior kinds
Must toil and bleed. But God, who gave so far
Dominion over them, extended not
The royal grant to torture or abuse:
And he who overtasks them, or inflicts
Protracted or unnecessary pain,
By far outstrips His warrant, and heaps up
On his own head for the great reckoning day
Such measure as he metes withal to them,
Of tender mercy. I would not devote
My person, as the pious Hindoo doth,
To banquet noxious vermin; nor engage
The patient carcass of some needy wretch
To make them pasture; nor abstain, like him,
From food of every kind that has contained
The living essence. I despise and loathe
The affected whine of canting sentiment,

That loves to expatiate on its own fine frame
Of exquisite perception—nerve all o'er—
Too tremblingly alive for the mind's peace
To every shade of delicate distress.
Such sensitives there are, whose melting souls
Dissolve in tender pity, or flame out
With generous indignation, if they see
A dog chastised, or noxious reptile crushed :—
Does a fly tease you, and with impulse quick
Your dexterous hand destroys the buzzing pest—
Prepare ye for an eloquent appeal
On the sweet duties of humanity,
And all the tender charities we owe
To the poor, pretty, little, helpless things
"That float in ether." Then some hackneyed verse—
Your sensitive must doat on poetry—
She quotes to illustrate the touching theme,
How "the poor beetle that we tread upon
In corporal sufferance feels a pang as great
As when a giant dies." 'Tis odious thus
To hear the thing one venerates profaned
By sickly affectation: to my ear
Doubly distasteful, for I heard the words
First from her lips whose heart was pity's throne.
That voice maternal taught my infant tongue
To speak the sentence, and my youthful heart
To feel and cherish, while its pulses beat,
Mercy and kindness for all living things.

Go where you will, the sensitive finds out
Whereon to expatiate largely—to pour forth
The flood of her pathetic eloquence.
A plodding clown to market drives along
His swine obstreperous : right and left they run

The Birthday.

In sheer perversity: so right and left
Resounds the whip, but scarcely reaches them,
Whate'er their horrid dissonance implies.
No matter—feeling's champion cannot hear
Unmoved the cry of innocence oppressed;
So forth she steps, and speaks, with hand on heart,
Tender remonstrance to the boor, who stands
Scratching his bushy pate, with hat pushed up,
And eyes and mouth distended with surprise,
Vented at last, when the oration ends,
In one expressive expletive—"Anan!"

A cart comes by—ah! painful sight indeed,
For it conveys, bound fast with cruel cords,
To the red slaughter-house a bleating load
Of fleecy victims. Now the impassioned soul .
Of sensibility finds ample scope
To excruciate its own feelings, and their hearts
Condemned to hear, while she minutely dwells
On things revolting—"How the murderous knife
Shall stop those bleating throats, and dye with gore
Those milk-white fleeces."
     Thus expatiates she,
While feeling turns aside, and hurries on.

But vulgar sufferings, 'mongst the vulgar part
Of our own species, often fail to excite
Those tender feelings that evaporate half
O'er flies and earwigs, and expend themselves
In picturesque affliction.
     "Ah!" cries one,
"How happy is the simple peasant's lot,
Exempt from polished life's heart-riving woes,
And elegant distresses!"

                                    Bid them turn—
Those sentimental chymics, who extract
The essence of imaginary griefs
From overwrought refinement,—bid them turn
To some poor cottage—not a bower of sweets
Where woodbines cluster o'er the neat warm thatch,
And mad Marias sing fantastic ditties,
But to some wretched hut, whose crazy walls,
Crumbling with age and dripping damps, scarce prop
The rotten roof, all verdant with decay;
Unlatch the door, those starting planks that ill
Keep out the wind and rain, and bid them look
At the *home-comforts* of the scene within.
There on the hearth a few fresh-gathered sticks,
Or smouldering sods, diffuse a feeble warmth,
Fanned by that kneeling woman's labouring breath
Into a transient flame, o'erhanging which
Cowers close, with outspread palms, a haggard form,
But yesterday raised up from the sick-bed
Of wasting fever, yet to-night returned
From the resumption of his daily toil.
"Too hastily resumed—imprudent man!"
Ay, but his famished infants cried for bread;
So he went forth and strove, till nature failed,
And the faint dews of weakness gathered thick
In the dark hollows of his sallow cheek,
And round his white-parched lips. Then home he
        crawled
To the cold comforts of that cheerless hearth,
And of a meal whose dainties are set out
Invitingly—a cup of coarse black tea,
With milk unmingled, and a crust of bread.
No infant voices welcome his return
With joyous clamour, but the piteous wail,

The Birthday. 47

"Father! I'm hungry—father! give me bread!"
Salutes him from the little huddled group
Beside that smoky flame, where one poor babe,
Shaking with ague-chills, creeps shuddering in
Between its mother's knees—that most forlorn,
Most wretched mother, with sad lullaby
Hushing the sickly infant at her breast,
Whose scanty nourishment yet drains her life.

Martyrs of sensibility! look there!
Relieve in acts of charity to those
The exuberance of your feelings.
                                    " Ay, but those
Are horrid objects—squalid, filthy, low
Disgusting creatures—sentiment turns sick
In such an atmosphere at such a sight.
True cottage children are delightful things,
With rosy dimpled cheeks, and clustering curls;
It were an interesting task to dress
Such pretty creatures in straw cottage-bonnets,
And green stuff gowns, with little bibs and aprons
So neat and nice! and every now and then,
When visitors attend the Sunday school,
To hear them say their catechism and creed.
But those!—oh heaven! what feelings could endure
Approach or contact with those dirty things?
True—they *seem* starving; but 'tis also true
The parish sees to all those vulgar wants;
And when it does not, doubtless there must be—
Alas! too common in this wicked world—
Some artful imposition in the case."

Martyrs of sensibility! farewell!
I leave ye to your earwigs and your flies.

But, gentle sportsman! yet a word with you
Ere to the starting-point I come again
From this long ramble unpremeditate.
Your sylvan sports you call most innocent,
Manly, and healthful. Are they always such?
Healthful I grant—for while the sons of sloth
Doze half their sleepy lives in morning dreams,
Ye are awake and stirring with the lark;
And like the lark ye meet on breezy hill,
In dewy forest glade, on perfumed heath
The breath of morning and her roseate smile.
Most healthful practice—and so far most pure.
But is it innocent, for murderous sport,
To scare sweet peace from her belovèd haunts?
To sadden and deface with death the scene
Where all breathes life, and love, and harmony?
And is it manly, with assembled rout
Of horses, dogs, and men, to hunt to death
A poor defenceless, harmless, fearful wretch,
The panting hare? For life—for life she flies,
And turns, and winds, and doubles in her course
With art instinctive—unavailing all.
Now the wild heath, the open plain she tries;
Now scuds for refuge to the pleasant brake,
Where many a morning she was wont to sit
In her old form, all spangled round with dew;
No rest—no respite—danger presses near—
'Tis at her heels. They burst the thicket now,
Yet still she moves not—for she cannot move;
Stiffened with terror, motionless she sits
With eyes wide staring, whence, I've heard some say,
Large tears roll down, and on her panting sides
The soft fur wet with dews of agony.
Finish the picture ye who list—I turn

The Birthday.

Disgusted from the task. But can I pass
Regardless the more lingering, torturing death
Too oft inflicted? We behold, indeed,
The furred and feathered trophies of his skill,
Disgorged from that fell gulf, the sportsman's bag;
Not pleasing to *all* hearts, I trow, the sight
Of even that lifeless spoil. But could we see—
Ah! could we follow to their sad retreats
Those more unhappy that escape with life,
But maimed and bleeding! To the forest depths
They crawl or flutter; there with dabbled plumes—
All stiff with clotted gore their burnished gold—
The graceful pheasant cowers beneath some tree,
Whose pleasant branches he shall mount no more.
Down droops the shattered wing, and crimson drops
Mark where the shot has entered in his breast.
There are no surgeons 'mongst the woodland tribes
To set such fractures—no purveyors there
To cater for the wounded, helpless bird;
Nay, his own species, with unnatural hate—
As if, like some of humankind, they feared
Contagion from approach to misery—
Drive the poor sufferer from their gay resorts;
So to some lonely nook he creeps away
To starve and die, abandoned and unseen.

Such wretched fate my little hare's had been,
But he, whose erring shot performed but half
Its deadly mission, brought it gently home
To be my guest and plaything, if it lived;
And to my loving care its life was given.
I nursed it fondly, every want and wish
Promptly contenting. So I won at last
Its grateful confidence; but not like those,

Beloved of Cowper, did my hare abide
Long after years in pleased captivity.
Nature prevailed; and when the prickly furze
Girdled our meadow with its golden belt
Of odorous blossoms, to that tempting brake,
Where harboured some of his own kind, my hare
Cast many a wistful look, as by my side
He leapt and frolicked in the garden near;
Yet long the powerful instinct he withstood
Prompting to liberty.   Compunctious thought
Perhaps it was of gratitude to me
That kept him still a prisoner on parole.

How oft in human hearts such strife springs up
'Twixt inclination and the scrupulous doubts
Of rigid conscience!   Bold at first, we cry,
"Satan, avaunt!" to the seducing fiend,
And he retires; but seldom in despair.
Wise by experience, close at hand lurks he,
Watching the time through some unguarded chink
To slip into the "swept and garnished" hold
Of his old citadel.   Perchance disguised
Like whispering Prudence, or in Feeling's mask,
Or Reason's pompous robe, he enters in.
Then Hesitation, with her shaking hand
And ever-shifting balance, weighs the cause;
And if a mote, a hair, a dust prepond—
No matter how it came there, or why left—
On Inclination's side, down drops the scale.

A cause less trivial fixed at last the fate
Of my poor Puss.   One morning by my side
In that same garden well content she sat
Nibbling some fresh-picked dainty, when, behold!

With horrid bark, in bursts a stranger dog—
One who had never learnt respect for hares—
And scents the victim; but in vain, for they
Who follow close restrain his savage speed,
And Puss escapes, o'erleaps the shallow fence,
And scuds across the mead, and safely gains
That prickly covert, which, beheld from far,
Had filled her heart with wandering wishes long.

From that day forth the hare, no longer mine,
Made her abode in that same hollow bank
Thick set with bushes, whence I saw her oft
Come forth at morn and even to sport and feed;
And oft the truant slave, the wild maroon,
With bold assurance leapt the garden fence
For purposes of plunder. Base return
For kind protection to her helpless state
So long accorded! nay, extended still
To shield her from the penalty of guilt;
For direful wrath in Ephraim's bosom rose—
The dragon he, whose guardianship had rule
Within the garden—when he found at morn
Traces yet recent of the plunderer's work.
His early lettuces all nibbled round,
And ranks of tender pease—his fondest pride!—
Laid down in patches, where the audacious thief,
Squatting composedly, had munched her fill.
Dire was the wrath of Ephraim!—much raved he
Of traps, and guns, and vengeance—whence restrained
By interdiction of the higher powers,
He muttered 'twixt his teeth reflections keen
About the blind indulgence of *some folk*
For children's whimsies—" Who could keep, forsooth,
A garden as it should be kept—not he—

The Birthday.

If noxious *varmint* was encouraged there?
What was the use of hares but for the spit?
He wished with all his heart that the whole race
Was killed and spitted. Everything he did
Was crossed and thwarted—mischief was at work
In every corner. If he could but *ketch*
Them folk that meddled when his back was turned
Among his mousetraps! 'Twas a thing unknown
That mousetraps should be set from day to day
With toasted cheese, and never catch a mouse."

Ah, friend! "there are more things in heaven and
    earth"
Than were dreamt of in *thy* philosophy.
Yet Ephraim had his shrewd suspicions too,
Though darkly hinted. There was *meaning* couched,
Though little terror in his threatenings vague;
For he too loved me well—the kind old man!
And would have torn from his own reverend head
The few white locks ere hurt a hair of mine.
Who but old Ephraim treasured up for me
The earliest strawberry, cunningly matured
On the red plane of sun-reflecting tile?
Who laid aside for me the longest string
Of clear white currants? With inviting smile,
Who dangled temptingly above my head
Twin cherries?—luscious prize! soon caught and won—
Who but old Ephraim, for his "little Queen,"
Picked out—his favourite emblem of herself—
The smallest pippin with the pinkest cheek?
It pleased him that I took delight to watch
His rural labours—that I asked the names
Of seeds and plants, and when to sow and set,
And their fixed season to bear flower and fruit.

The Birthday. 53

With patient seriousness he made reply
To questions multiplying faster still
Than he could answer. But it puzzled oft
His honest head—no learned Pundit he—
To solve the curious questions I proposed,
Why such and such things were; to which most part
One answer served—incontrovertible,
Oracular—"they were, because they were."
Oh! what a deal of mischief were unmade
If Ignorance always on perplexing points
Replied as prudently—if folks at least
Pretended to teach only what they know.
Young ladies! how especially for you
'Twould simplify the training! No she-Crichtons,
No petticoat professors would engage
To teach all 'OLOGIES and 'OGRAPHIES,
And everything in all the world—of course
Accomplishments included—all complete
In all their branches. What a load of rubbish,
Now crammed, poor dears! into your hapless brains,
Would leave the much abusèd organ room
To expand, and take in healthful nutriment.

Wise, honest Ephraim! Shall I leave unsung
Thy skill in fashioning small wooden toys,
Small tools, adapted to my pigmy grasp?
His hand is eagerly stretched out on whom
Fortune bestows a sceptre; his no less
To whom she gives the baton of command,
The marshal's truncheon; and she smiles herself
At his more solemn transport, from beneath
The penthouse of enormous wig, who eyes
The seals of office dangling in his reach.
And bearded infants—babies six feet high,

The Birthday.

Scramble for glittering baubles; ribbons, stars,
And garters, that she jingles on a pole
For prizes to the foremost in the race,
Or who leaps highest, or with supplest joints
Who twists, and turns, and creeps, and wriggles best.
But none with greater eagerness than I
From Ephraim's hand received the finished spade
Whose small dimension might have served at need
Some kitchen damsel for a tasting spoon,
Albeit proportioned aptly for my use;
And other tools he fashioned, rakes and hoes,
And oh! sublime perfection of his craft,
Most precious specimen! his genius last
Shaped out a wheelbarrow, and I attained,
Possessed of that long-coveted machine,
The climax of my wishes. What delight
To cram it with such offsets, plants, and bulbs
As Ephraim from his own neat borders cast;
Then to wheel off the load, no matter what,
To my own garden. Nought came then amiss
Or out of season. Scions of tall trees,
And bushy shrubs, that, had they taken root
And flourished, would have filled the small domain;
And ragged pinks, with huge old scraggy roots,
Past hope of e'er producing flower or bud,
And plants full blown, that nothing lacked—but roots.

But not unfrequently the wheelbarrow
Was freighted with a living, yelping load—
Old Chloe's puppies: she the while, poor fool!
Trotting beside with anxious look and whine
Much eloquent of wonder and dismay
And half displeased remonstrance, at the enforced
And early travels of her progeny.

The Birthday.

Many there are among Creation's Lords
Whom Fashion wheels abroad—a listless load!—
As blind and senseless as those noisy whelps,—
As blind to all the wonders in their way
Of Art and Nature: with as senseless noise
Chattering among themselves their mother-tongue
In foreign lands, disdaining to acquire
The useless knowledge—spiritless pursuit!—
Of a strange people's customs, arts, and speech;
And who return with minds as unenlarged,
And skulls as empty, to their native land,
As to their kennel Chloe's brood returned.
But they, poor innocents! were safe restored,
With simple unsophisticated minds;
While two-legged puppies bring a cargo home
Of affectation, pedantry, and vice.

It is not all who having eyes can see,
Or having ears can hear: that truth we learn
From everyday experience. How it frets
One's soul to be associated with those
Deaf hearers, blind beholders! Frets one more,
That all the outward organs they possess,
As it appears, unblemished. So we're led
To utter freely what we warmly feel;
And then it proves that all the wires and pipes
That should communicate 'twixt eyes and ears
And the indwelling Soul, to empty cells
Lead only, sending back response nor sound.

Say with a friend we contemplate some scene
Of natural loveliness, from which the heart
Drinks in its fill of deep admiring joy;
Some landscape scene, all glorious with the glow

Of summer evening, when the recent shower,
Transient and sudden, all the dry white road
Has moistened to red firmness; every leaf,
Washed from the dust, restored to glossy green;—
In such an evening oft the setting Sun,
Flaming in gold and purple clouds, comes forth
To take his farewell of our hemisphere;
Sudden the face of Nature brightens o'er
With such effulgence, as no painter's art
May imitate with faint similitude.
The rain-drops dripping fast from every spray
Are liquid topazes; bright emeralds those
Set on the green foil of the glistening leaves,
And every little hollow, concave stone,
And pebbly wheel-track, holds its sparkling pool
Brimming with molten amber. Of those drops
The Blackbird lights to drink; then scattering thick
A diamond shower among his dusty plumes,
Flies up rejoicing to some neighbouring elm,
And pours forth such a strain as wakens up
The music of unnumbered choristers.
Thus Nature to her great Creator hymns
An hallelujah of ecstatic praise.
And are *our* voices mute? Oh, no! we turn,
Perhaps with glistening eyes, and our full heart
Pours out in rapturous accents, broken words,
Such as require no answer, but by speech
As little measured, or that best reply,
Feeling's true eloquence, a speaking look.
But other answer waits us; for the *friend*—
Oh, heaven! that there are such—with a calm smile
Of sweet *no-meaning*, gently answers—"Yes,
Indeed it's very pretty—Don't you think
It's getting late, though—time to go to tea?"

The Birthday.

Some folks will tell you, of all things on earth
They most like reading; poetry with them
Is quite a passion; but somehow it is,
They never find a moment's leisure time
For things they dote on.   What a life is theirs!
There's the new poem—they would give the world
To skim it over, but it cannot be;
That trimming must be finished for the ball.
If *you indeed*, who read aloud so well,
With so much feeling, would but take the book—
'Twould be so *nice* to listen! such a treat!
And all the while the trimming might go on.
You cannot have the heart to disappoint
Wishes expressed so sweetly.   Down you sit
But unreluctant to the task, which soon
Absorbs your every feeling.   'Tis perhaps
Of Roderick, that immortal Goth, you read—
Immortalised in verse that cannot die
Till Poesy is dead, and every heart
Warmed with her sacred fire a senseless clod.

The first few pages smoothly on you go,
Yourself delighted, and delighting much—
So simply you believe—your hearers too.
At length a whisper, audibly aside,
Or 'cross the table, grates upon your ear,
And brings you from the region of romance—
"Dear! how provoking! have you seen my thread?—
No—here it is—Oh! pray don't stop—go on
With that delightful story."
                                On you go;
But scarce recover from that first rude shock,
When lo! a second.   Deep debate ensues,
Grave, solemn, nice, elaborate, profound,

About the shade of some embroidered leaf,
Whether too dark—or not quite dark enough—
Or whether *pea* green were not after all
Fitter than *apple* green. And there you sit
Devoutly banning in your secret soul
Balls, trimmings, and your own too easy faith
In sympathy from hearers so engrossed.
"Better leave off," you say, and close the book,
"Till some more leisure morning."—But at once
All voices clamour at the barbarous thought
Of such adjournment:—And you recommence,
Loath and disheartened; but a lull succeeds
Of seeming deep attention, and once more
The noble song absorbs you, heart and soul.
That part you reach, where the old Dog who lies
Beside Rusilla, and, unnoticed, long
Has eyed the dark-cowled Stranger; all at once,
Confirmed by Love's strong instinct, crawls along
And crouches at his royal Master's feet,
And licks his hand, and gazes in his face
"With eyes of human meaning."
       Then—just then—
When trembling like a harp-string to the touch
Of some impassioned harmonist, your voice
Falters with strong emotion—
       "Oh!" cries she,
The passion of whose soul is poesy,
"That dear sweet dog!—It just reminds me, though,
That poor Tonton was washed two hours ago,
And I must go and comb him, pretty love!
So for this morning, though it breaks my heart,
From that dear book I tear myself away."
Ah, luckless reader! wilt thou e'er again
On such as these expend thy precious breath?

The Birthday.

Some travelled exquisites profess a taste—
"Gusto," they call it—for the sister art—
For painting. Heaven preserve us from such taste!
These learnedly harangue on breadth and depth,
Gradation, concentration, keeping, tone,
Tint, glazing, chiaroscuro, and what not.
At some old picture—moderns cannot paint—
Some smoke-dyed canvass, where experienced eyes
In the brown chaos may distinguish form,
Lo! where they gaze with reverential awe,
Peer through the focus of their rounded hand,
With features screwed up to the exactest pitch
Of connoisseurship—fall enraptured back,
With head aside, and eyes all puckered up
Obliquely glancing—then with folded arms
They stand entranced, and gaze, and sigh, and gaze,
And mutter ecstasies between their teeth—
"Divine! incomparable! grand! unique!"

Less learned critics condescend to admire
Some amateur production—yours perhaps;
These, little skilled in jargon technical
Of conoscenti, murmur gentle praise.
Holding your drawing to their eyes quite close,
As 'twere a newspaper, and they perplexed
To make out the small print, "Dear me!" they cry,
"How nice! how natural! how very soft!"
These phrases serve, or some as richly fraught
With meaning, for all subjects and all styles;
Or, if with more discriminating taste,
They own a preference, it falls, be sure,
On the most worthless, whose tame character
Is in this gentle phrase—"So very soft!"

The Birthday.

Inflict not on me, Stars! the killing blight
Of such companionship. Oh! rather far
Assign me for my intimate and friend
One who says plainly, "I confess to me
Painting's but coloured canvass, music noise,
And poetry prose spoilt, those rural scenes
Whereon *you* gaze enraptured, nothing more
Than hill and dale and water, wooded well
With stout oak timber groaning for the axe."

'Twixt such a heart and mine there must be still
A bar, oft painfully perceived indeed,
And never overstepped: But I could feel
Respect—affection—confidence for such,
If dignified with sound clear-judging sense
And piety, that gem beyond all price,
Wherewith compared all gifts are valueless.

It is not once an age two hearts are set
So well in unison that not a note
Jars in their music; but a skilful hand
Slurs lightly over the discordant tones,
And wakens only the full power of those
That sound in concord.
                        Happy, happy those
Who thus perform the grand concerto—Life!

The Birthday.

PART THE THIRD.

CONTENTS.

The Old Milestone.—Angling.—Royden Stream.—The Sylvan Feast.
—Age of Intellect.—Afternoon.—Isaac Walton.—A Bitter Night.—
The Farmer.—The Pet Lamb.—Our Old Garden.—Painting.—The
Altar.—Priscilla.—Tea-Drinking.—Curiosities.—The Cuckoo Clock.
—William Gilpin.—The Visit.—The Vicarage.—The Study.

OLD friend! old stone! old way-mark! art thou gone?
I could have better spared a better thing
Than sight of thy familiar shapeless form,
Defaced and weather-stained. But thus it is
Where'er I turn me, wheresoe'er I look,
Change, change, change, change, is everywhere at work
In all mine ancient haunts. Grammercie, though!
Reform—improvement, is the proper word.
We live, God wot! in an improving age,
And our old world, if it last long enough,
Will reach perfection. Lo! conceptions vast
Germ not alone in patriot statesman's mind
Or great philanthropist's. *Our* public men—
Ours in this rural district nook o' the world,
"Armed with a little brief authority,"
Wield it like Jove's own thunder, and affect
The Olympic nod. Would they had nodded off
Their sapient heads, ere, in an evil hour,
Beautiful elms! your spreading branches fell,
Because, forsooth, across the King's highway,
Conspiring with the freeborn, " chartered " air,
Your verdant branches treasonably waved,
And swung perchance the pendant dewdrops off

On roof of royal mail, or in the eyes
Of sleepy coachman, wakened so full well
For safety of his snoring "four insides,"
Unconscious innocents!—or on *his* pate—
His awful pate—even his, mine ancient foe,
Your ruthless enemy—the man of power,
Of measurement, and Acts of Parliament,
The great road dragon—man of flinty heart—
Belike ye showered the liquid crystal down,
Irreverend boughs! and so your fate was sealed.
But, veteran oak! what rank offence was thine?
In memory of man thou hadst not flung
One flickering shadow 'thwart the royal road,
Nor intercepted sunbeam from the head
Of noontide traveller. Only left of thee
The huge old trunk, still verdant in decay
With ivy garlands, and a tender growth—
Like second childhood—of thine own young shoots;
And there, like giant guardian of the pass,
Thou stoodst, majestic ruin! thy huge roots,
Whose every fretted niche and mossy cave
Harboured a primrose, grappling the steep bank,
A wayside rampart. Lo! they've rent away
The living bulwark now—a ghastly breach,
A crumbling hollow left to mark its site
And the proud march of utilitarian zeal.

And the old thorns are gone—the thorns I loved,
For that in childhood I could reach and pluck
Their first sweet blossoms. They were low, like me;
Young, lowly bushes—I a little child;
And we grew up together. They are gone:
And the great elder by the mossy pales—
How sweet the blackbird sang in that old tree!

The Birthday.

Sweeter, methinks, than now, from statelier shades—
They've felled that too, the goodly, harmless thing!
That with its fragrant clusters overhung
Our garden hedge, and furnished its rich store
Of juicy berries for the Christmas wine,
Spicy and hot, and its round hollow stems,
The pith extracted, for quaint arrow-heads,
Such as my father in our archery games
Taught me to fashion. That they've ta'en away,
And so some relic daily disappears,
Something I've loved and prized; and now the last—
Almost the last—the poor old milestone falls,
And in its place this smooth, white, perked-up thing,
With its great staring figures.
      Well, well, well!
All's doubtless as it should be. Were *my* will
The rule of action, strange results, I doubt,
Would shock the rational community.
No farmer round should clip one straggling hedge,
No road-surveyor change one rugged stone,
Howe'er illegible its lettered face,
Nor pare, nor trim, nor chop one craggy bank,
Nor lop one wayside tree, although its boughs
Arched all the royal road. I'd have the road
One bowery arch—what matter if so low
No mail might pass beneath? For aught I care
The post might come on foot, or not at all,
At least with tidings of the troublous world.
In short—in short, it's quite as well, perhaps,
I can but rail—not rule. Splenetic words
Will not tack on again dissevered boughs,
Nor set up the old stone; so let me breathe
The fulness of a vexèd spirit out
In impotent murmurs.

The Birthday.

Gentles, could you guess
What thoughts, what feelings, what remembrances
Are in my mind associated with sight
Of that cold senseless stone, that shapeless thing
Which there lies postrate, ye would smile perhaps,
But not methinks in *scornful* wonderment
At the strange utterings of my wayward mood.
Here, to this very spot, the guardian hand
Still clasping mine, with tottering steps I came,
A good half mile from home—my first *long* walk—
The first remembered. Here, the goal attained,
They set me up on the old stone to rest,
And called me woman!—Baby now no more,
Who walked so stoutly; filled my lap with flowers,
And pulled within my reach the woodbine down,
That I might pluck, with mine own eager hand,
A wreath for Dido's neck. She sat beside,
The grave old creature, with her large brown eyes
Intently, as in delegated watch,
Fixed on her master's child. Soon came the days,
When *his* companion—his, his only one,
My father's—I became. Proud, happy child!
Untiring now in many a lengthened walk,
Yet resting oft, his arm encircling me,
On the old milestone in our homeward way.

My father loved the patient angler's art;
And many a summer day, from early morn
To latest evening, by some streamlet's side
We two have tarried. Strange companionship!
A sad and silent man—a joyous child.
Yet were those days, as I recall them now,
Supremely happy. Silent though he was,
My father's eyes were often on his child,

The Birthday.

Tenderly eloquent, and his few words
Were kind and gentle. Never angry tone
Repulsed me, if I broke upon his thoughts
With childish question. But I learnt at last,
Learnt intuitively, to hold my peace
When the dark hour was on him, and deep sighs
Spoke the perturbed spirit: only then
I crept a little closer to his side,
And stole my hand in his, or on his arm
Laid my cheek softly, till the simple wile
Won on his sad abstraction, and he turned
With a faint smile, and sighed, and shook his head,
Stooping toward me: so I reached at last
Mine arm about his neck, and clasped it close,
Printing his pale brow with a silent kiss.

That was a lovely brook, by whose green marge
We two, the patient angler and his child,
Loitered away so many summer days!
A shallow sparkling stream, it hurried, now
Leaping and glancing among large round stones,
With everlasting friction chafing still
Their polished smoothness, on a gravelly bed
Then softly slipped away with rippling sound,
Or all inaudible where the green moss
Sloped down to meet the clear reflected wave
That lipped its emerald bank with seeming show
Of gentle dalliance; in a dark, deep pool
Collected now, the peaceful waters slept,
Embayed by rugged headlands, hollow roots
Of huge old pollard willows. Anchored there,
Rode safe from every gale a sylvan fleet
Of milk-white water-lilies, every bark
Worthy as those on his own sacred flood

The Birthday.

To waft the Indian Cupid. Then the stream
Brawling again o'er pebbly shallows ran,
On, on to where a rustic, rough-hewn bridge,
All bright with mosses and green ivy wreaths,
Spanned the small channel with its single arch;
And underneath the bank on either side
Shelved down into the water, darkly green
With unsunned verdure, or whereon the sun
Looked only when his rays at eventide
Obliquely glanced between the blackened piers
With arrowy beams of orient emerald light
Touching the river and its velvet marge.
'Twas there, beneath the archway, just within
Its rough misshapen piles, I found a cave,
A little secret cell—one large flat stone
Its ample floor, imbedded deep in moss,
And a rich tuft of dark blue violet;
And fretted o'er with curious groining dark,
Like vault of Gothic chapel, was the roof
Of that small cunning cave—"The Naiad's Grot"
I named it learnedly, for I had read
About Egeria, and was deeply versed
In heathenish stories of the guardian tribes
In groves, and single trees, and sylvan streams
Abiding co-existent. So methought
The little Naiad of our brook might haunt
That cool retreat, and to her guardian care
My wont was ever, at the bridge arrived,
To trust our basket, with its simple store
Of home-made, wholesome cates, by one at home
Provided for our banquet-hour at noon.

A joyful hour! anticipated keen,
With zest of youthful appetite I trow,

The Birthday.

Full oft expelling unsubstantial thoughts
Of Grots and Naiads, sublimated fare.
The busy, bustling joy, with housewife airs—
Directress, handmaid, lady of the feast—
To spread that "table in the wilderness"!
The spot selected with deliberate care,
Fastidious from variety of choice,
Where all was beautiful: some pleasant nook
Among the fringing alders, or beneath
A single spreading oak, or higher up
Within the thicket, a more secret bower,
A little clearing, carpeted all o'er
With creeping strawberry, and greenest moss
Thick veined with ivy.   There unfolded smooth
The snowy napkin, carefully secured
At every corner with a pebbly weight,
Was spread prelusive—fairly garnished soon
With the contents, most interesting then,
Of the well-plenished basket: simple viands,
And sweet brown bread, and biscuits for dessert,
And rich, ripe cherries; and two slender flasks,
Of cyder one, and one of sweet new milk,
Mine own allotted beverage, tempered down
To wholesome thinness by admixture pure
From the near streamlet.   Two small silver cups
Set out our grand buffet—and all was done.
But there I stood immovable, entranced,
Absorbed in admiration, shifting oft
My ground contemplative to reperuse
In every point of view the perfect whole
Of that arrangement, mine own handiwork.
Then glancing skyward, if my dazzled eyes
Shrank from the sunbeams, vertically bright,
Away, away, toward the river's brink

I ran to summon from his silent sport
My father to the banquet, tutored well,
As I approached his station, to restrain
All noisy outbreak of exuberant glee,
Lest from their quiet haunts the finny prey
Should dart far off to deeper solitudes.
The gentle summons met observance prompt,
Kindly considerate of the famished child:
And all in order left; the mimic fly
Examined and renewed, if need required,
Or changed for other sort, as time of day,
Or clear or clouded sky, or various signs
Of atmosphere or water, so advised
The experienced angler; the long line afloat,
The rod securely fixed, then into mine
The willing hand was yielded, and I led
With joyous exultation that dear guest
To our green banquet-room. Not Leicester's self,
When to the hall of princely Kenilworth
He led Elizabeth, exulted more
With inward gratulation at the show
Of his own proud magnificence, than I,
When full in view of mine arrangèd feast,
I held awhile my pleased companion back,
Exacting wonder, admiration, praise,
With pointing finger, and triumphant "There!"

Our meal concluded—or, as Homer says,
" Soon as the rage of hunger was appeased "—

And by the way, our temperate sylvan feast
Deserved poetic illustration more
Than those vast hecatombs of filthy swine,
Where Trojans, Greeks, and half-immortals gorged,

The Birthday.

Sharpening their wits for council. Process strange!
But most effectual, doubtless, as we see
Clearly illustrated in this our day,
In this our favoured isle, where all affairs
(Glory to Britain's intellectual age!)
Begin and end with feasting. Statesmen meet
To eat and legislate; to eat and hang [1]
Judges assemble; chapters congregate
To eat and order spiritual affairs;
Philhellenists to eat and free the Greeks;
Committees of Reform, Relief, Conversion,
Eat with amazing unction : and so on,
Throughout all offices, sects, parties, grades,
Down to the Parish worthies, who assemble [2]
In conclave snug to eat, and starve the poor.

Our banquet over—nor omitted then
Grateful acknowledgment for good received
From Him whose open hand all living things
" Filleth with plenteousness "—my dear companion
Sought once again the river's flowery marge,
To me committing—as the spreading out—
The gathering up all fragments of the feast,
" That nothing might be lost." Instruction wise,
By simple illustration well enforced ;
Nor strained to Pharisaic meaning hard,
Forbidding to communicate the good
Abundantly bestowed. So liberal dole
I scattered round for the small feathered things
Who from their leafy lodges all about
Had watched the strange intruders and their ways,
And eyed the feast with curious wistfulness,
Half longing to partake. Some bold, brave bird,
He of the crimson breast, approaching near

The Birthday.

And near and nearer, till his little beak
Made prize of tempting crumb, and off he flew
Triumphant, to return—permitted thief—
More daringly familiar.
                       Neatly packed
Napkin and cups, with the diminished store
Of our well-lightened basket; largess left
For our shy woodland hosts; some special treat
In forkèd branch or hollow trunk for him,
The prettiest, merriest, with his frolic leaps
And jet-black sparkling eyes, and mimic wrath
Clacking loud menace—yet before me lay
The long bright summer evening. Was it long,
Tediously long, in prospect? Nay, good sooth!
The hours in Eden never swifter flew
With Eve yet innocent, than fled with me
Their course by thy fair stream, sweet Royden Vale!

The stream, the mead, herb, insect, flower, and leaf,
Sunbeam and shadow, all, as I have said,
Were books to me, companionable things;
But lack of other volume, Man's device,
Was none, when, turning from the outspread scroll
Of beauteous Nature, sweet repose I sought
In varied pleasure. In a certain pouch,
Ample and deep, the Fisher's coat within,
Lurked an old clumsy russet-covered book,
That with permitted hand extracted thence—
(I *see* the smile to the young smiling thief
Vouching impunity)—for many an hour
Furnished enjoyment, flavoured not the less
For oft renewed experience intimate.
Just where the river with a graceful curve
Darkened and deepened in the leafy gloom

The Birthday.

Of a huge pollard oak, a snug retreat
I found me at the foot of that old tree,
Within the grotto-work of its vast roots,
From whose fantastic arches, high upheaved,
Sprang plumy clusters of the jewelled fern,
And adder's-tongue, and ivy wreaths hung down
Festooning elegant, soft greenest moss
Flooring the fairy cave, the tempered light,
As through an emerald roof, stole gently in,
Caressingly, and played in freckling gleams
On the dark surface of the little pool,
Where as it seemed the lingering stream delayed
As loath its brawling course to recommence
In glaring sunshine. Ah! could *we* delay
Time's current, as it bears us through some reach
Where the rough stream sinks waveless, peace-embayed!

The river at my feet, its mossy bank
Clipped by that caverned oak, my pleasant seat,
Still as an image in its carved shrine
I nestled in my sylvan niche, like hare
Upgathered in her form, upon my knees
The open book, o'er which I stooped intent,
Half-hidden, the large hat flung careless off,
In a gold gleaming shower of auburn curls.
Ah, gentle Isaac! by what glamourie
Chained ye the eyes of restless childhood down
To pages penned for other readers far,
Mature and manly? What concern of mine
Thy learnèd lessons to the docile twain,
Thy some time pupils? What concern of mine
Thy quaint directions how to dress a chub?
Or bait the barbèd hook with hapless frog,
  " Lovingly handled"? What concern of mine

The Birthday.

Thy merry meetings at that rural hostel
With the fair hostess—lavender in the window,
And "twenty ballads stuck about the wall"?
Yet sure I longed to share of that same chub,
And took no thought how that unlucky frog
Relished such loving treatment; and full fain
Would have made one at that same merry board,
And drank in with insatiate ear thy words,
Rich in the truest wisdom, for throughout,
(Hallowing whate'er of homely, quaint, and coarse
Might shock fastidious taste, less pure than nice),
The love of God, and Man, and holy Nature
Breathed like the fragrance of a precious gum
From consecrated censer. Then those scraps
From the olden poets—"the divine Du Bartas,"
And "holy Master Herbert," and Kit Marlowe,
Whose ballad by the modest Milkmaid sung
Combined methought sweet strain of sweetest bird,
And pleasant melody of trickling rill,
And hum of bees, and every natural tone
Most musical. And then what dear delight
Beneath the sheltering honeysuckle hedge
To share thy leafy covert, while "the shower [3]
Fell gently down upon the teeming earth,
From the green meadows all with flowers bedecked
Wakening delicious odours; while the birds'
Friendly contention, from a grove hard by,
Held with an echo, whose dead voice did live—
So seeming—in a hollow tree high up
Crowning the primrose knoll." Ah, gentle Isaac!
How could I choose but love thy precious book,
Then in that blessed springtime of my life
When life was joy, this fair earth paradise,
And thine a master-key, in its green glades

Opening innumerous paths! I love thee still
With an exceeding love, old battered book!
And from thy time-discoloured leaves outsteal
Methinks sweet breathings of that merry May
So long o'erpast. My Winter is at hand—
Summer departed, Autumn on the wane—
But as I read, and dream, and smile, and sigh,
Old feelings stir within me, old delights
Kindle afresh, and all the past comes back
With such a rush, as to its long-dried bed
The waters of a stream for many a year
Pent from its natural course.
      Oh! nothing dies—
Nothing is lost or wholly perisheth
That God hath callèd good, and given to Man,
Worth his immortal keeping. Let them go,
Let them pass from me like a troubled dream,
The things of this world; bitter apples all,
Like those by the Dead Sea, that mock the eye
With outward fairness, ashes at the core.
Let this frail body perish day by day,
And to the dust go down, and be resolved
Thereunto—earth to earth: but *I* shall live
In spiritual identity unchanged,
And take with me where happy spirits dwell
(Through Christ, the door, I hope admittance there)
All thoughts, desires, affections, memories
Sealed with the heavenly stamp, and set apart—
Made worthy—for duration infinite.

"This is a bitter night for the young lambs,"
My father said, and shivering drew his chair
Close in to the warm hearth. "The biting air,
When I looked out but now, was thick with snow

The Birthday.

Fast driven in furious gusts—and hark ! that's hail
Clattering against the window."
                                To the storm
Listening a moment, with a pitying thought
For houseless wanderers, to our dear fireside
We turned with grateful hearts, and sweetest sense
Of comfort and security, that each
Reflected in the other's face, read plain
As in a page of some familiar book
Long learned by heart.
                      "Cary ! what makes you sigh
And look so sad i' th' sudden ? " asked my mother,
As, letting fall my pencil, I rose up,
And, stealing to my father's side, drew close
The little stool, my own peculiar seat,
And, leaning on his knee, looked earnest up,
With that long deep-drawn breath, that ends so oft
Childhood's reflective pause.
                             " I'm thinking, mother,
Of what my father said about the lambs—
What *will* become of them this bitter night,
Poor little pretty creatures ? We looked at them
A long, long while, on our way home to-day,
While with their mothers they were folded up
By the old shepherd. Some could hardly stand,
So very weak they were, so very young !
Don't you remember, father ! you said then
A cold hard night would kill them."
                                   " Did I, child ?
Well, this is cold enough. But then the shepherd
Will take good heed to them—and——Little girl !
Have you not heard, and read, and learnt, how God
' Tempers the wind to the shorn lamb ' ? So these,
Helpless and tender as they are, His eye
Still watcheth, and His guardian care protects."

The Birthday.

"Oh! but I wish"——unuttered was the wish;
For the door opened, and a burly form,
Much like a walking bear, the hairy cap,
And shaggy wrapping coat, all white with snow,
Announced by baying house-dogs, and shown in
With little form by Joe, within the room
Advanced a step or two, in country fashion,
Scraping obeisance. Up sprung old Di,
With hostile growling, from her master's feet;
But sniffing round the stranger, in a moment
Dropping her tail, she came contented back
To her warm station.
     "What's the matter, Farmer,
That you're abroad so late this blusterous night?"
My father, with a friendly greeting, asked;
"My little lassie, here, was just bewailing
For your young lambs—but they're all snug, I guess."

"Ay, ay, sir! thank ye kindly, snug enough;
And many thanks to Miss, God bless her heart!"
He added, with a loving look at me,
Who had stolen round by this to my old friend,
Admiring much his bruin-like aspect.
A knowing twinkle with that loving look
Was mingled; and his bluff good-natured face
Brightened with kindliness, as he went on:—

"I'll lay my life on't, Miss will never guess
What I've got here, all cuddled up so warm
Under my old greatcoat. And yet, Lord love her!
The *thing's* for her, whatever it may be!"

Then there was wonder and impatient joy,
And jumping round and round, and

"Oh, dear Farmer!
Is it alive?—what is it?—*let* me look—
Only *one* peep."—And eagerly I pulled
At the wet shaggy coat.
               "Just let me *feel!*"
Then with feigned caution he admitted slow
One little curious hand.
               "How soft—how warm!—
It's a young kitten!"
               "Kitten!—sure I'd scorn
To bring such vermin."
               "Well, a rabbit, then—
Or—no—I'm sure now it's a guinea-pig—
Isn't it, Farmer?"
               "Guinea pigs don't bleat—
Hearken!"
               "Oh mercy!—it's a little lamb!"

"My Missis said 'twas just the thing for Miss,
When Amos brought it in an hour agone
From the dead ewe. The poor dumb brute had three,
This only living; well enough for strength,
Considering: and Miss will mud* it up,
I know, as clever as a little queen,
If I may leave it for her."
               If!—that if
Checked in a moment my ecstatic fit,
And a quick glance imploringly I turned
To the parental faces. Smiles were there,
But not consenting ones—and heads were shaken,
And sage remonstrance was preparing plain,
And lips were opened; but I stopt them quick

* Mud—Provincial.

With smothering kisses, and—the lamb was mine.
And thanks to Lydia, maiden most expert
In things pertaining to the dairy's charge,
And country matters—ever mine ally,
Ready and faithful—the small creature throve
As though the mother's milk and her strong love—
Nature's unerring course—had nurtured it;
And from a tender fondling, soon became
My mate and playfellow. Such friends we were—
Willy and I! Inseparable friends,
In door and out—up-stairs and down—where'er
My step was heard, the little pattering hoofs
Close following, or before me, sounded too.
Only at lesson time awhile disjoined
The fond companionship. Good reason why—
The pupil never much renowned at best
For patient application; little chance
Was there of any, when that gamesome thing
Made scoff of learning, and its teachers grave;
Upsetting inkstands—nibbling copy-books—
And still provoking to irreverent mirth
With some new merry mischief.
                              Time went on—
More wondrous had he stopt—and winsome Willy,
The pet lamb still, drew near to ram's estate—
Then 'gan affairs to alter. Budding horns,
Fondled at first, grew formidable things,
And pretty freedoms to audacious onslaughts.
Old Di was sent off howling—from the lines
  Linen hooked down and tattered—maids laid
    sprawling—
And visitors attacked, and butchers' boys,
And bakers, with their trays and baskets, butted,
And forced to fly and hallo for their lives.

Our mutual love still perfect, I alone
'Scaped molestation, threatening life or limb;
Only for summer wear more cool and airy
The muslin frocks were made, by sundry slits
From top to bottom, and large eyelet holes;
But that was all in sport—no harm intended—
And I the last to take offence at things
Concerning only those who had to mend
Or to replace my wardrobe. But all hearts
Were not so placable, and day by day
Dark looks and angry murmurs darker grew,
And waxed more wrathful.
      " 'Twas not to be borne:
The beast was dangerous: some serious mischief
Would come of it at last ; it must be seen to."
O Willy! Willy! how I quaked for fear
At those vague threatenings, with ingenious art
Concealing or excusing as I could
Thine oft delinquencies. But all in vain ;
The fatal day, long dreaded, came at last.
It was the time of blossoms, and my father,
Who in " trim gardens " much delight did take,
Was scanning with a gardener's prideful eye
His neat espaliers ; every well-trained branch
Thick set with bloom—deep blushing like the morn,
Or fainter tinged, or snow-white, of each sort
Indicative, and its abundant fruit. Fair show!
Rich promise! Many a season cold, unkind,
Had nipped the gardener's hope since such was
  seen—
" If frost returns not, and no cruel blight
Comes near us"—with exultant hope broke forth
My father's meditation—when, alas!
Destruction was at hand, and in mid speech

The Birthday.

He stopt astounded. Frost nor blight most dire
So direful as the sight of visible mischief
Personified in Willy's form, at work
Ten paces off, where thick as snowflakes fell
A shower of milk-white blossoms. Glorious sport!
Another butting charge, and down they come,
Whitening the walk and border.
      "Help! help! help!
Ho, Ephraim! Ephraim!" At the call appear
More than the summoned—rushes out amain
The gaping household, mistress, maids, and man,
And I, half guilty, much confounded cause
Remote, of all the evil, helpless then
To stay its progress.
     "Here he is—here! here!
Stop him—he's off again!"
      "Where? where?" "There, there!"
Down comes the flowery rain—that shake will do
For the old golden rennet—fair pearmain!
Thy turn comes next—and next—
       "Destruction! death!
There goes the gansels bergamy—will no one
Stop the cursed brute?"
       How beautiful he looked!—
Even in my shame and terror so I thought—
When at safe distance he stood still and gazed
At his pursuers with provoking air
Of innocent wonder, dangling from his mouth
A bunch of apple blossoms, now and then
Mumbled in wantonness.
      "Confound him! there!
He's at the golden pippin. Where's the gun?
Joe! run and fetch it—or—hold, hold—a rope!
We'll noose the rascal!"

The Birthday.

        Oh, my heart! my heart!
How died ye at the sound of guns and ropes!
But capture was not death; and he was caught—
Caught and led up to judgment. Willy! Willy!
That ever to such strait and to such woe
Thine evil courses should have brought us both!
For the decree went forth that parted us,
Thou to return to thy first owner's flock,
And I, bereaved, to mourn my merry mate.
Ah, doleful day! when for the last, last time
We two went forth together, thou, poor fool!
In thine unconscious gladness by my side
Trotting contentedly, though every step
Took thee to exile nearer, and my tears
Fell fast as summer raindrops. How I clung,
When to the farm we came, with sobbing clasp
About thy snowy neck, refusing comfort,
Although they told me, to assuage my grief,
A many flattering tales of good designed,
Peculiar good to thee. Thou wert to range
For life respected, master of the flock,
To crop the sweetest herbage, and be housed,
When winter came, in warm luxurious crib.
"But shall I see him sometimes?"
          "Ay, ay, sure,
Often and often, when the flock comes back
From the far pastures."
       Back it came—alas!
I saw not Willy—saw him never more;
But half deluded still by glozing words,
I thought not, witless! of the butcher's cart,
Nor transmutation fell, by murderous sleight,
Of sheep to mutton. To thy manes peace,
Offending favourite, wheresoe'er thy grave!

The Birthday.

Dear garden! once again, with lingering look,
Reverted, half remorseful, let me dwell
Upon thee as thou wert in that old time
Of happy days departed. Thou art changed,
And I have changed thee. Was it wisely done?
Wisely and well, they say who look thereon
With unimpassioned eye, cool, clear, undimmed
By moisture such as memory gathers oft
In mine, while gazing on the things that are,
Not with the hallowed past, the loved, the lost,
Associated as those I now retrace
With tender sadness. The old shrubbery walk,
Straight as an arrow, was less graceful far
Than this fair winding among flowers and turf,
Till with an artful curve it sweeps from sight
To reappear again, just seen and lost
Among the hawthorns in the little dell.
Less lovely the old walk; but there I ran
Holding my mother's hand, a happy child;
There were her steps imprinted, and my father's,
And those of many a loved one, now laid low
In his last resting-place. No flowers, methinks,
That now I cultivate are half so sweet,
So bright, so beautiful, as those that bloomed
In the old formal borders. These clove pinks
Yield not such fragrance as the true old sort
That spiced our pot-pourri, my mother's pride,
With such peculiar richness; and this rose,
With its fine foreign name, is scentless, pale,
Compared with the old cabbage—those that blushed
In the thick hedge of spiky lavender,
Such lavender as is not nowadays;
And gillyflowers are not as they were then,
Sure to "come double;" and the night breeze now

Sighs not so loaded with delicious scents
Of lily and sevinger. Oh, my heart!
Is all indeed so altered?—or art thou
The changeling, sore aweary now at times
Of all beneath the sun?
                            Such weariness
Knows not that blessed spring-time of the heart
When "treasures dwell in flowers." How glad was I,
How joyously exultant, when I found
Such virtues in my flowery treasury
As hitherto methought discoverer's eye
Had passed unheeded! Here at once I found,
Unbought, unsued for, the desired command—
How longingly desired!—of various dyes,
Wherewith to tint the semblance incomplete
In its hard pencil outline, of those forms
Of floral loveliness, whose juices now
Supplied me with a palette of all hues,
Bright as the rainbow. Brushes lacked I none
For my rude process, the soft flower or leaf
Serving for such; its moisture nice expressed
By a small cunning hand, where'er required
The imitative shadow to perfect
With glowing colour. Heavens! how plain I see,
Even at this moment, the first grand result
Of that occult invention. *There* it lies,
Living as life itself (I thought no less),
A sprig of purple stock, that dullest eye
Must have detected, and fault-finding critic
Have owned at least a likeness. Mother's love
Thought it perfection, when with stealing step
And flushing face and conscious, I drew near,
And laid it on her lap without a word,
Then hung upon her shoulder, shrinking back

The Birthday.

With a child's bashfulness, all hope and fear,
Shunning and courting notice.
      But I kept
Profoundly secret certain floral rites
Observed with piously romantic zeal
Through half a summer. Heaven forgave full sure
The unconscious profanation; and the sin,
If sin there was, be on thy head, old friend,
Pathetic Gesner! for thy touching song,
That most poetic prose, recording sad
The earliest annals of the human race,
And death's first triumph, filled me, heart and
  brain,
With stirring fancies, in my very dreams
Exciting strange desires to realise
What to the inward vision was revealed,
Haunting it like a passion. For I saw,
Plain as in substance, that first human home
In the first earthly garden;—saw the flowers
Set round her leafy bower by banished Eve,
And watered with her tears, as they recalled
Faintly the forfeit Eden; the small rills
She taught to wander 'mongst their blooming tribes,
Completing, not the semblance, but the shade.
But beautiful, most beautiful, methought
The altar of green turf, whereon were laid
Offerings as yet unstained with blood—choice fruits,
And fairest flowers fresh culled.
      "And God must still"—
So with myself I argued—"surely love
Such pure, sweet offerings. There can be no harm
In laying them, as Eve was wont, each day
On such an altar. What if I could make
Something resembling that!" To work I went,

With the strong purpose which is strength and power;
And in a certain unfrequented nook
Of our long rambling garden, fenced about
By thorns and bushes, thick with summer leaves,
And threaded by a little watercourse—
No substitute contemptible, methought,
For Eve's meandering rills—uprose full soon
A mound of mossy turf, that when complete
I called an altar; and with simple faith,
Ay, and with feelings of adoring love
Hallowing the childish error, laid thereon
Daily my floral tribute; yet from prayer,
Wherewith I longed to consecrate the act,
Refraining with an undefinèd fear,
Instinctive of offence: and there was doubt
Of perfect blamelessness, unconscious doubt,
In the suspicious, unrelaxing care
With which I kept my secret. All's not well,
When hearts, that should be open as the day,
Shrink from inspection. So by slow degrees
I grew uneasy and afraid, and longed
To cast off the strange burden; and at last,
Ceasing my visits to "the sacred grove,"
I soon forgot, absorbed in fresh pursuits,
The long-neglected altar—till one day,
When coming winter, with his herald blasts,
Had thinned the covert's leafiness, I saw
Old Ephraim in his clearing progress pause,
And strike his spade against a mossy heap,
Washed low by autumn's rains, and littered round
Among the thick-strewn leaves with spars and shells,
And broken pottery, and shrivelled things
That had been garlands.

The Birthday.

"This is Missy's work,"
Quoth the old man, and shook his head, and smiled;
"Lord bless her! how the child has toiled and moiled
To scrape up all this rubbish. Here's enough
To load a jackass!"
                    Desecrated shrine!
Such was thy fate, demolished as he spoke;
And of my Idyl the concluding page.

"The Thane of Fife," said some one, "hath a wife;"
And so had Ephraim—a precise old dame,
Looking like ancient waxwork; her small face,
Of lemon-coloured hue—framed closely round
With most elaborate quilling—puckered up
To such prim fixedness, the button mouth
Scarcely relaxed into a button-hole
When with a smile distended; and the eyes,
Two small black beads, but twinkled, never moved.
And mincing was her speech, and picked withal,
Dainty and delicate, as was her frame,
Like an old fairy's. She had spent her youth,
And prime, and middle age—two-thirds of life—
In service of a maiden gentlewoman
Of the old buckram sort, wellnigh extinct,
Prudent, and formal, and fantastical,
Much given to nervous tremors and hysterics,
Flutterings and qualms, and godly books, and tales
Of true love crossed, and dreams, and pious courtship.
Of that soft sisterhood was Mistress Martha,
On one-legged bullfinches and wheezing lapdogs
Who lavish sympathies long run to waste,
"Since that unhappy day"—'twas her own phrase,
Mysterious, unexplained—oft hinted at
In memory's melting mood to faithful Prissey,

With sighs deep fetched, and watery upturned eyes
Glancing unutterable things, where hung,
Enshrined in shagreen case, a miniature,
Set round with garnets, in a true-love knot
Wreathed at the top, the portraiture within
Of a slim, pink-and-white young gentleman
In bag and solitaire, and point cravat,
With a peach-blossomed coat—"Ah, Prissey! Prissey!
Good girl! remember"—so the lady still
Addressed her handmaiden, when forty years
And five, full told, her girlhood had matured—
" Men are deceivers all—put no faith in them ;
But live and die a chaste and peaceful maid."
With decent grief Priscilla to the grave
Followed her monitress, and that day month
To Ephraim (who had waited for his wife
With patriarchal patience), nothing loath,
Plighted her virgin troth.
      Came with the bride
Into her husband's long-prepared home,
In carved oak chest, and trunks with gilded nails,
Curiously flourished, store of household stuff,
And goodly raiment—of the latter, much
Unfitting wear for decent humble folk
Knowing their station, as full well did they,
Keeping thereto with sense of self-respect,
Insuring that of others. But Priscilla,
A favoured handmaiden, and privileged,
Accustomed long to copy, half unconscious,
Her lady's speech, and habits, and attire—
(I well remember now her puffed-out kerchief,
Closed with a garnet pin, her black fringed mits,
And narrow velvet collar)—thought no wrong
On Sundays, and on suitable occasions,

The Birthday.

To come forth, awful to the cottage children,
In rustling pomp of some grave coloured lustring,
Sprigged muslin apron, short black satin cloak,
A thought embrowned with age, but handsome still,
Edged round with rabbit skin, and on her head,
By long black pins secured to cap and cushion,
A bonnet—Mistress Martha's second best—
A velvet skimming-dish, flounced round with lace
Darned to a double pattern. Then her shoes!
Black velveteen, high-heeled, with silver buckles:
So in her glory did Priscilla shine
On holidays and high days. Then her wits,
In housewifery expedients rich, were taxed
To cut, convert, turn, twist, transmogrify
Incongruous elements to useful ends.
Triumph of female skill!—as by enchantment,
Even at the waving of the magic shears,
Sacks, petticoats, and negligees became
Waistcoats and breeches. Shade of Mistress Martha!
Saw ye the desecration? So on Sundays,
Donning brocaded vest, and nether garment
Quilted like wise King Jamie's, warm and rich,
His good drab broadcloth coat, with basket buttons,
Heired from his grandsire, making all complete
Of Ephraim's outward man, forth sallied he,
Doing discredit none to her whose eye
Glanced sidelong approbation, as they took
Leisurely, arm in arm, the churchward way.
No scholarship had Ephraim. A plain man,
Plain spoken, chary of his words, was he,
But full of reverence for Priscilla's claims
To knowledge, learning, and superior breeding.
Deep read was she in varied lore profound,—
Divinity, Romance, and Pharmacy,

And—so the neighbours whispered—in *deep* things
Passing the Parson's wisdom. Store of books,
The richest portion of the bridal dower,
Were ranged in goodly order on two shelves,
The third and topmost with choice porcelain piled,
Surmounting an old walnut-tree bureau;
The Holy Bible, cased in green shaloon,
And Book of Common Prayer, a fine black type,
Were laid conspicuous on the central spot,
As first in honour; flanked on either side
By 'Taylor's Golden Grove,' 'The Pilgrim's Progress,'
And 'Fox's Book of Martyrs.' How I loved
To ransack those old tawny, well-thumbed leaves,
Supping my fill of horrors! Sermons too,
Discourses hydra-headed, had their place,
And 'Hervey's Meditations 'mongst the Tombs,'
With courtly Grandison and 'Pamela,'
All full of cuts—supreme delight to me!
And the true history—sweetly scented name!—
Of Jemmy and fair Jenny Jessamy.

Then came a ragged row of Magazines,
And songs, and hymn-books; 'Kettlewell on Death,'
And 'Glass's Cookery.' Treatises abstruse
On moles and warts, and virtues of all herbs,
And ailments manifold that flesh is heir to.
What wonder if respect akin to awe
For her who owned and *studied* those grave tomes
Impressed the simple neighbours? For myself—
Unblushingly I do confess it now—
Not without tremor, half delight, half fear,
I entered, clinging to the Nursemaid's hand,
Through the clipt laurel porch, that small neat room,
So nicely sanded round the clean-swept hearth,

The Birthday.

Where sat expectant—(Mistress Jane, I trow,
Had her appointments for occult discourse
And cup of fragrant Hyson)—the wise woman,
With her strange primmed-up smile, the round claw table
Set out before her with its precious freight
(In Sheffield tea-tray) of old *real* china,
The sugar-basin a scooped cocoa-nut
Curiously carved all o'er and ebon-stained,
On three small toddling silver feet, rimmed round
With the same precious metal; silver tongs
Stuck for effect among the sparkling knobs,
With two thin tea-spoons of the treasured six;
There on its trivet the bright kettle sang,
Its cheek all ruddy with rich firelight glow;
And piping hot the buttered oven-cake
Smoked on the fender ledge, all ready quartered.
Inviting preparations not alone
To black-eyed Jane: the treat had charms for me
More irresistible;—that buttered cake!—
Forbidden dainty—tea with cream and sugar!
True, but *just* finished was my nursery meal—
Dry bread and milk and water. "What of that?
The precious lamb had walked a weary way,
And sure must need refreshment. One small piece
Of nice hot buttered cake would do her good,
And tea, a saucerful, to wash it down."
So urged the Dame: Jane shook her head and smiled—
Conscience made faint resistance—the rich steam
Rose fragrant to my nostrils, and—I fell.

My treat despatched, the Maid and Matron turned
To whispered consultation, leaving me,

Right glad, to seek amusement as I would.
No lack of that, though I had stayed for hours.—
There was the cat and kitten—always *one*,
A creature of immortal kittenhood,
For whom, suspended by a worsted thread
To knob of dresser drawer, a bobbing cork
Dangled, perpetual plaything; there aloft
Among the crockery stood a small stuffed pug,
Natural as life, tight curled-up tail and all,
And eyes that glared a snarl; and there i' the sun
A venerable one-eyed cockatoo
With gouty legs, snored dozing in his cage—
A sacred trust! by dying lips consigned,
With his life income, to Priscilla's care.
Then there were prints and pictures hung all round—
Prints of the Parables, and one rare piece,
A landscape—castles, clouds, trees, men, and sheep,
All featherwork! Priscilla when she died
Bequeathed it to me. Poor old harmless soul!
That ever half-afraid I should have shrunk,
Scarce knowing why, from one who loved me kindly:
But then she looked so strangely, and they said
Such strange things of her.
                          Well! and then—and then—
There was the 'Book of Martyrs,' and 'The Pilgrim,'
And fifty other rarities and treasures;
But chief—surpassing all—a cuckoo clock!
That crowning wonder! miracle of art!
How have I stood entranced uncounted minutes,
With held-in breath, and eyes intently fixed
On that small magic door, that when complete
The expiring hour—the irreversible—
Flew open with a startling suddenness
Which, though expected, sent the rushing blood

The Birthday.

In mantling flushes o'er my upturned face;
And as the bird—that more than mortal fowl!—
With perfect mimicry of natural tone,
Note after note exact time's message told,
How my heart's pulse kept time with the charmed voice!
And when it ceased made simultaneous pause
As the small door clapt to, and all was still.

Long did I meditate—yea, often dream
By day and night, at school-time and at play,—
Alas! at holiest seasons, even at church
The vision haunted me,—of that rare thing,
And his surpassing happiness to whom
Fate should assign its fellow. Thereupon
Sprang up crude notions, vague incipient schemes
Of future independence: not like those
Fermenting in the youthful brain of her
Maternally, on fashionable system,
Trained up betimes i' the way that she should go
To the one great end—a good establishment.
Yet similar in some sort were our views
Toward contingent power. "When I'm a woman
I'll have," quoth I,—so far the *will* and *when*
Tallied exactly, but our difference lay
Touching the end to be achieved. With me,
Not settlements, and pin-money, and spouse
Appendant, but in unencumbered right
Of womanhood—a house and cuckoo clock!

Hark! as I hang reflective o'er my task,
The pen fresh nibbed and full, held idly yet;
What sound comes clicking through the half-closed door,
Distinct, monotonous?—'Tis even so;
Years past, the pledge, self-plighted, was redeemed;

The Birthday.

There hangs with its companionable voice
The cuckoo clock in this mine house.—Ay, *mine;*
But left unto me desolate. Such end
Crowns oft Ambition's most successful aim—
Success than disappointment more defeating;—
Passionate longing grasps the ripened fruit
And finds it marred, a canker at the core:
What shall I dare desire of earthly good
The seeming greatest; what in prayer implore
Or deprecate, of that my secret soul
In fondness and in weakness covets most
Or deepest dreads, but with the crowning clause,
The sanctifying—" Lord! Thy will be done?"

Farther a-field we journeyed, Jane and I,
When summer days set in, with their long, light
Delicious evenings. Then, most happy child!
Most favoured!—I was sent a frequent guest,
Secure of welcome, to the loveliest home
Of all the country, o'er whose quiet walls
Brooded the twin-doves, Holiness and Peace:
There with thine aged partner didst thou dwell,
Pastor and master! servant of thy Lord,
Faithful as he, the labours of whose love
Recorded by thy pen, embalm for aye
The name of Gilpin heired by thee—right heir
Of the saint's mantle. Holy Bernard's life,
Its apostolic graces unimpaired,
Renewed in William's, virtuous parish priest!

Let me live o'er again, in fond detail,
One of those happy visits. Leave obtained,
Methought the clock stood still. Four hours past noon,
And not yet started on our three mile walk!

The Birthday.

And *six* the vicarage tea hour primitive,
And I should lose that precious hour, most prized,
When in the old man's study, at his feet,
Or nestling close beside him, I might sit
With eye, ear, soul intent on his mild voice,
And face benign, and words so simply wise
Framed for his childish hearer. "Let us go!"
And like a fawn I bounded on before,
When lagging Jane came forth, and off we went.
Sultry the hour, and hot the dusty way,
Though here and there by leafy screen o'erarched—
And the long broiling hill! and that last mile
When the small frame waxed weary! the glib tongue
Slackening its motion with the languid limbs.
But joy was in my heart, howe'er suppressed
Its outward show exuberant; and, at length,
Lo! the last turning—lo! the well-known door,
Festooned about with garlands picturesque,
Of trailing evergreens. Who's weary now?
Sounding the bell with that impatient pull
That quickens Mistress Molly's answering steps
To most unusual promptness. Turns the lock—
The door uncloses—Molly's smiling face
Welcomes unasked. One eager, forward spring,
And farewell to the glaring world without;
The glaring, bustling, noisy, parched-up world!
And hail repose and verdure, turf and flowers,
Perfume of lilies, through the leafy gloom
White gleaming; and the full, rich, mellow note
Of song-thrush, hidden in the tall thick bay
Beside the study window!
                            The old house,
Through flickering shadows of high-arching boughs,
Caught gleams of sunlight on its time-stained walls,

And frieze of mantling vine; and lower down,
Trained among jasmines to the southern bow,
Moss roses, bursting into richest bloom,
Blushed by the open window. There she sate,
The venerable lady, her white hair
White as the snowy coif, upon her book
Or needlework intent; and near at hand
The maiden sister friend—a lifelong guest—
At her coarse sempstresship—another Dorcas,
Unwearying in the work of charity.

Oh! kindest greeting! as the door unclosed
That welcomed the half-bold half-bashful guest,
And brought me bounding on at a half word
To meet the proffered kiss. Oh, kindest care!
Considerate of my long, hot, dusty walk,
Of hat and tippet that divested me,
And clinging gloves; and from the glowing cheek
And hot brow, parted back the clustering curls,
Applying grateful coolness of clear lymph,
Distilled from fragrant elder—sovereign wash
For sunburnt skin and freckled! Kindest care,
That followed up those offices of love
By cautionary charge to sit and rest
" *Quite still* till tea time." Kindest care, I trow,
But little relished. Restless was my rest,
And wistful eyes, still wandering to the door,
Revealed " the secret of my discontent,"
And told where I would be. The lady smiled,
And shook her head, and said,—
                              " Well! go your ways
And ask admittance at that certain door
You know so well." All weariness was gone—
Blithe as a bird, thus freed, away I flew.

The Birthday.

And in three seconds at the well-known door
Tapped gently; and a gentle voice within
Asking "Who's there?" "It's *me*," I answered low,
Grammatically clear. "Let *me* come in,"
The gentle voice rejoined; and in I stole,
Bashfully silent, as the good man's smile,
And hand extended, drew me to his chair;
And there all eye and ear, I stood full long,
Still tongueless, as it seemed; love-tempering awe
Chaining my words up. But so kindly his,
His aspect so benign, his winning art
So graciously conforming; in short time
Awe was absorbed in love, and then unchained
By perfect confidence, the little tongue
Questioned and answered with as careless ease
As might be, from irreverent boldness free.
True love may cast out fear, but not respect,
That fears the very shadow of offence.

How holy was the calm of that small room!
How tenderly the evening light stole in,
As 'twere in reverence of its sanctity!
Here and there touching with a golden gleam
Book-shelf or picture-frame, or brightening up
The nosegay set with daily care—love's own—
Upon the study table. Dallying there
Among the books and papers, and with beam
Of softest radiance, starring like a glory
The old man's high bald head and noble brow,
There still I found him, busy with his pen—
Oh pen of varied power! found faithful ever,
Faithful and fearless in the one great cause—
Or some grave tome, or lighter work of taste—

His no ascetic, harsh, soul-narrowing creed—
Or that unrivalled pencil, with few strokes,
And sober tinting slight, that wrought effects
Most magical—the poetry of art!
Lovely simplicity!—true wisdom's grace—
That, condescending to a simple child,
Spread out before me hoards of graphic treasures;
Smiling encouragement as I expressed
Delight or censure—for in full good faith
I played the critic—and vouchsafing mild
To explain or vindicate; in seeming sport
Instructing ever; and on graver themes
Winning my heart to listen, as he taught
Things that pertain to life.
      Oh precious seed!
Sown early; soon, too soon—the sower's hand,
The immediate mortal instrument withdrawn—
Tares of this evil world sprang thickly up
Choking your promise. But the soil beneath—
Nor rock nor shifting sand—retained ye still,
God's mercy willing it, until *His* hand,
Chastening as fathers chasten, cleared at last
The encumbered surface, and the grain sprang up.—
But hath it flourished?—hath it yet borne fruit
Acceptable? Oh Father! leave it not
For lack of moisture yet to fall away!

THE LEGEND OF SANTAREM.

COME listen to a monkish tale of old,
 Right Catholic, but puerile some may deem,
Who all unworthy their high notice hold
 Aught but grave truth, or lofty learnèd theme ;
Too wise for simple fancies, smiles, and tears,
Dreams of our earliest, purest, happiest years.

Come, listen to my legend ; for of them
 Surely thou art not : and to thee I'll tell
How on a time in holiest Santarem
 Strange accident miraculous befell
Two little ones, who to the sacred shrine
Came daily to be schooled in things divine.

Twin sisters—orphan innocents were they :
 Most pure, I ween, from all but the olden taint,
Which only Jesu's blood can wash away :
 And holy, as the life of holiest saint,
Was his, that good Dominican's, who fed
His Master's lambs, with more than daily bread.

The children's custom, while that pious man
 Performed the various duties of his state
Within the spacious church, as sacristan,
 Was on the altar steps to sit and wait,
Nestling together ('twas a lovely sight !)
Like the young turtle-doves of Hebrew rite.

The Legend of Santarem.

A small rich chapel was their sanctuary,
  While thus abiding;—with adornment fair
Of curious carvèd work, wrought cunningly,
  In all quaint patterns and devices rare:
And over them, above the altar, smiled
From Mary-Mother's arms, the Holy Child:

Smiled on His infant guests, as there below,
  On the fair altar steps, those young ones spread—
Nor aught irreverent in such act, I trow—
  Their simple morning meal of fruit and bread.
Such feast not ill beseemed the sacred dome—
Their Father's house is the dear children's home.

At length it chanced, upon a certain day,
  When Frey Bernardo to the chapel came,
Where patiently was ever wont to stay
  His infant charge, with vehement acclaim,
Both lisping creatures forth to meet him ran,
And each to tell the same strange tale began.

"Father!" they cried, as, hanging on his gown
  On either side, in each perplexèd ear
They poured their eager tidings—"He came down—
  Menino Jesu has been with us here!—
We asked Him to partake our fruit and bread;
And He came down—and sate with us—and fed."

"Children! my children! know ye what ye say?"
  Bernardo hastily replied. "But hold!—
Peace, Briolanja!—rash art thou alway:
  Let Inez speak." And little Inez told,
In her slow silvery speech, distinctly o'er,
The same strange tidings he had heard before.

The Legend of Santarem.

"Blessed are ye, my children!" with devout
　　And deep humility the good man cried.
"Ye have been highly favoured. Still to doubt
　　Were gross impiety and sceptic pride.
Ye have been highly favoured. Children dear!
Now your old master's loving counsel hear.

"Return to-morrow with the morning light,
　　And, as before, spread out your simple fare
On the same table; and again invite
　　Menino Jesu to descend and share:
And if He come, say, 'Bid us, blessed Lord!
We and our master, to Thy heavenly board.'

"Forget not, children of my soul! to plead
　　For your old master:—Even for *his* sake
Who fed ye faithfully: and He will heed
　　Your innocent lips; and I shall so partake
With His dear lambs. Beloved! with the sun
Return to-morrow.—Then—His will be done."

"To-night! to-night! Menino Jesu saith
　　We shall sup with Him, Father! we and thee,"
Cried out both happy children in a breath,
　　As the good Father entered anxiously,
About the morrow's noon, that holy shrine,
Now consecrate by special grace divine.

"He bade us come alone; but then we said
　　We could not, without thee, our master dear.
At that, He did not frown, but shook His head
　　Denyingly: Then straight with many a tear
We prayed so sore, He could not but relent,
And so He smiled at last, and gave consent."

The Legend of Santarem.

"Now, God be praised!" the old man said, and fell
    In prayer upon the marble floor straightway,
His face to earth: and so, till vesper-bell,
    Entrancèd in the spirit's depths he lay;
Then rose like one refreshed with wine, and stood
Composed among the assembling brotherhood.

The mass was said; the evening chant was o'er;
    Hushed its long echoes through the lofty dome:
And now Bernardo knew the appointed hour
    That he had prayed for, of a truth was come.
Alone he lingered in the solemn pile,
Where darkness gathered fast from aisle to aisle;

Except that through a distant doorway streamed
    One slanting sunbeam, gliding whereupon
Two angel spirits—so in sooth it seemed
    That loveliest vision—hand in hand came on,
With noiseless motion. "Father! we are here,"
Sweetly saluted the good Father's ear.

A hand he laid on each fair sun-bright head,
    Rayed like a seraph's with effulgent light,
And—"Be ye blest, ye blessed ones," he said,
    "Whom Jesu bids to His own board to-night.
Lead on, ye chosen; to the appointed place
Lead your old master." So, with steadfast face,

He followed where those young ones led the way,
    To that small chapel. Like a golden clue
Streamed on before that long bright sunset ray,
    Till at the door it stopt. Then passing through,
The master and the pupils, side by side,
Knelt down in prayer before the Crucified.

The Legend of Santarem.

Tall tapers burnt before the holy shrine ;
   Chalice and paten on the altar stood,
Spread with fair damask. Of the crimson wine
   Partaking first alone, the living food
Bernardo next with his dear children shared—
Young lips, but well for heavenly food prepared.

And there we leave them. Not for us to see
   The feast made ready, that first act to crown ;
Nor to peruse the solemn mystery
   Of the divine Menino's coming down
To lead away the elect, expectant three,
With Him that night at His own board to be.

Suffice it that with Him they surely were
   That night in Paradise ; for those who came
Next to the chapel found them as in prayer,
   Still kneeling, stiffened every lifeless frame,
With hands and eyes upraised as when they died,
Toward the image of the Crucified.

That mighty miracle spread far and wide,
   And thousands came the feast of death to see ;
And all beholders, deeply edified,
   Returned to their own homes more thoughtfully,
Musing thereon : with one great truth imprest—
That "to depart and be with Christ is best."

THE PAUPER'S DEATHBED.

TREAD softly—bow the head—
   In reverent silence bow—
No passing bell doth toll,
Yet an immortal soul
      Is passing now.

Stranger! however great,
   With lowly reverence bow;
There's one in that poor shed—
One by that paltry bed,
      Greater than thou.

Beneath that beggar's roof,
   Lo! Death doth keep his state:
Enter—no crowds attend;
Enter—no guards defend
      This palace gate.

That pavement damp and cold
   No smiling courtiers tread;
One silent woman stands
Lifting with meagre hands
      A dying head.

No mingling voices sound—
   An infant wail alone;
A sob suppressed—again
That short deep gasp, and then
      The parting groan.

Sonnet.

Oh, change ! oh, wondrous change !
  Burst are the prison bars :
  This moment *there*, so low,
  So agonised, and now
      Beyond the stars !

Oh, change ! stupendous change !
  There lies the soulless clod ;
  The Sun eternal breaks—
  The new Immortal wakes—
      Wakes with his God !

SONNET.—1818.

AUTUMNAL leaves and flowerets ! lingering last—
  Pale sickly children of the waning year !
A lovelier race shall yet succeed ye here,
When Nature, her long wintry torpor past
O'er the brown woods and naked earth doth cast
  Her vernal mantle. From its prison cell,
  Through mould and bark, the struggling germ shall swell,
Bright buds, and beauteous blossoms, following fast—
Oh ! I was wont a deep delight to taste,
  When the first primrose reared her modest head,
And early violet on the wintry waste,
  The renovated soul of sweetness shed !
And they will wake again—and I shall be,
Mine own belovèd home ! far, far from them and thee !

CONTE A MON CHIEN.

COME, my old Dog! come hither now,
   And rest thine head upon my knee,
And let us talk together: thou
   Hast something much at heart I see.

Ay, let them laugh who understand
   No utterance save of human speech—
We have a language at command
   They cannot feel, we cannot teach.

Yes, thy dark eye informeth mine
   With sense than words more eloquent:
Thy very ears, so long and fine,
   Are flexibly intelligent.

Come hither, then, my Dog! and rest
   Thy poor old head upon my knee,
And tell me why, with looks distrest,
   Thou eyest me so reproachfully.

Donna? the cat? Old fool! is she
   The object of thy jealous fears?
Fie, Ranger! ill becometh thee
   Such fancies at thy sober years.

Think'st thou that I remember not
   Thy dearer claims of days "lang syne"?
Can "auld acquaintance be forgot,"
   And love, and worth, and faith like thine?

What though I smooth her velvet fur,
  Whose mottled hues so finely blend?
What though I coax and fondle her?
  She's but a favourite—*thou* my friend.

And though thy ears, once glossy brown,
  Are faded now; though hoary white
With age's frost thy nose is grown,
  And dull thy hearing and thy sight;

And though thy once fleet limbs resign
  Their spring, then light as air-blown feather;
I love thee more for every sign
  That tells how long we've lived together.

And still thine eye is quick to see,
  To know me yet far off: thine ear
(Oh love-supplied deficiency!)
  Is keen *my* voice, *my* step to hear.

And still thou com'st with wild misrule,
  As in past time, to welcome me:
And yet thou think'st, old jealous fool!
  That that dull thing can rival thee.

Dost thou e'er hear me summon her
  To be companion of my walk?
Dost thou e'er hear me talk to her,
  As thou and I are wont to talk?

"But, mistress! on your lap she lies,
  While I am crouching at your feet:
And I've looked on with envious eyes,
  And seen her from your fingers eat."

Conte à mon Chien.

Now, my good friend! can thoughts arise
  So senseless in such brains as thine?
Compare thine own with Donna's size,
  And just reflect that cats must dine.

Look at that huge thick paw—and see,
  Thy wrist is larger round than mine:
Would'st thou a lady's nursling be?
  "But, mistress! why need puss be thine?"

Because she's gentle and polite,
  And small, and soft, and clean withal—
Whilst *thou*, for gown of purest white,
  Good friend! hast no respect at all.

Thou know'st in every muddy hole
  'Tis thy delight to dive and play—
Fresh from such sport, from head to sole,
  You splashed me o'er but yesterday;

While puss is always clean and sweet.
  "Ay, mistress! ay, small chance have I:
Your poor old servant at your feet,
  Despised, may lay him down and die.

"Yet I've been young, and comely too,
  And oft you've kissed my sleek brown head."
Nay, Ranger! if you take it *so*,
  I wish the cat was hanged and dead.

There, Ranger! there! you've won the field:
  The foe's expelled; art thou at peace?
Beshrew the heart that would not yield
  Indulgence e'en to love's caprice!

Conte à mon Chien.

Have I not told thee, faithful friend!
That good and evil, joy and pain,
We'll share until our journey's end?
That only death shall part us twain?

And never shall thy latter days
   Know want or suffering, wrong, distress,
That love, in all its countless ways,
   Can remedy, relieve, redress.

And thou shalt live out *all* thy life—
   No murderous hand shall lay thee low:
Forestalling time's more tedious strife,
   With *merciful, preventing* blow.

Their mercy shall not end thy "pain,"
   As they are pleased brute age to call:
No, thou shalt live, old friend! to drain
   Life's mingled potion, dregs and all.

And many a sweet that time defies,
   Even with the latest drops shall blend,
And many a comfort I'll devise
   To gild thy latter days, old friend!

Plenteous and soft thy bed shall be,
   Heaped up in basket warm and snug,
And thou shalt stretch luxuriously,
   Just in the centre of the rug;

And none shall chase thee thence, nor chide
   As now thy restless wanderings—no;
Scratch when thou wilt, the door flung wide
   Shall yield thee passage to and fro.

Just *here*, thy basket they shall bring,
   Before the early sunbeams fly;
Where, after many a measured ring,
   Coiled up at last, thou lov'st to lie.

And never shall thy poor dim eyes
   For tempting morsel ask in vain—
Never, if I can help it, rise
   In thine old heart one jealous pain.

Well! art thou satisfied, old friend?
   Are all thy foolish fancies fled?
" Ay, mistress! till——" I comprehend;
   Till next time puss is coaxed and fed.

But come, we've worn this theme to tatters,
   And all my logic's thrown away;
So let's discourse on other matters—
   And first—I've read a tale to-day.

Thou know'st whate'er I see, read, learn,
   Relating to thy species, friend,
I tell thee, hoping it may turn
   To thine advantage—so attend,

My good old Ranger! while I tell
   A true and mournful history,
How in past time it once befell
   A little faithful dog like thee.

'Twas in a neighbouring land: what time
   The Reign of Terror triumphed there:
And every horrid shape of crime
   Stalked out from murder's bloody lair:

And every fair and stately town
  Became a slaughter-house and grave,
Where fell prescription hunted down
  The good, the loyal, and the brave:

'Twas in those dreadful times there dwelt
  In Lyons, the defiled with blood,
A loyal family, that felt
  The earliest fury of the flood.

Wife, children, friends, it swept away
  From wretched Valrive, one by one:
Himself severely doomed to stay
  · Till everything he loved was gone—

A man proscribed, whom not to shun,
  Was danger, almost *fate*, to brave:
So all forsook him, all save one,
  One humble, faithful, powerless slave,

His dog, old Nina. She had been,
  When they were boys, his children's mate:
His gallant Claude, his mild Eugene,
  Both gone before him to their fate.

And she had followed mournfully
  Their parting steps; and when the door
Closed after them, it seemed as she
  Had *felt* they would return no more.

And when the dismal tidings came
  That they had perished in their bloom—
Blighted, cut off without their fame,
  Both huddled in one bloody tomb—

And heart-struck in her first despair
    The mother sank into her grave,
And Valrive, as he laid her there,
    Scarce wished he had the power to save;

But gazed upon that little heap,
    Safe shelter for the weary head,
And envied her untroubled sleep,
    And longed to share her peaceful bed:

Then as he stood beside the grave,
    With tearless eye, and lip compressed,
Crept to his feet his poor dumb slave,
    And moaned as if his thoughts she guessed;

And looked up in his face, and sighed
    As if her poor old heart would break;
And in her fond mute language cried,
    "Oh, master! live for Nina's sake."

They spurned her off—but ever more,
    Surmounting e'en her timid nature,
Love brought her to the prison-door,
    And there she crouched, fond, faithful creature!

Watching so long, so piteously,
    That e'en the jailer—man of guilt,
Of rugged heart—was moved to cry,
    "Poor wretch! there enter, if thou wilt."

And who than Nina more content,
    When she had gained that dreary cell,
Where lay in helpless dreariment
    The master loved so long and well!

And when into his arms she leapt,
  In her old fond, familiar way,
And close into his bosom crept,
  And licked his face—a feeble ray

Of something—not yet comfort—stole
  Upon his heart's stern misery;
And his lips moved, " Poor loving fool!
  Then *all* have not abandoned me."

The hour by grudging kindness spared
  Expired too soon—the friends must part—
And Nina from the prison fared,
  With lingering pace and heavy heart.

Shelter, and rest, and food she found
  With one who, for the master's sake,
Though grim suspicion stalked around,
  Dared his old servant home to take.

Beneath that friendly roof, each night
  She stayed, but still returning day—
Ay, the first beam of dawning light—
  Beheld her on her anxious way

Towards the prison, there to await
  The hour, when through that dismal door
The keeper, half compassionate,
  Should bid her enter as before.

And well she seemed to comprehend
  The time apportioned for her stay:
The little hour that with her friend
  She tarried then, was all her day.

But what an age of love, and grief,
    And confidence, was crowded in it!
How many a long, long life is brief,
    Compared with such a heart-fraught minute!

Methinks, old Ranger, thou and I
    Can fancy all they thought and said—
Believ'st thou not, of days gone by
    Their hearts communed, and of the dead?

Ay, on my life!—And Valrive spoke
    (The childless father!) of his boys
To their old playmate, and awoke
    The memory of their infant joys.

For ever thus, when in their prime
    A parent's hopes in dust are laid,
His heart recurs to that sweet time
    When, children, round his knees they played.

So oft in Nina's ear was breathed
    The names of those belovèd ones,
And hers, who could not live bereaved
    Of both her children.—Many suns

Went down upon the dreary pile
    Where Valrive lay—and evermore,
Punctual as light's returning smile,
    Came Nina to the prison-door.

At last the captive's summons came:
    They led him forth his doom to hear;
No tremor shook his thrice-nerved frame,
    Whose heart was dead to hope and fear.

Conte à mon Chien.

So with calm step he moved along,
  And calmly faced the murderous crew :
But close and closer for the throng,
  Poor Nina to her master grew.

And she has found a resting place
  Between his knees—her old safe home—
And she looks round in every face,
  As if to read his written doom.

There is no mercy but above—
  The word goes forth—the fatal breath—
Does instinct, or more powerful love,
  Tell thee, poor brute! that word is death?

Howe'er informed, a child might see
  The sentence struck upon her heart,
And that her eye's keen misery
  Said, "Master! we will never part."

'Twas but a step, in those dread days,
  From trial to the guillotine—
A moment—and Valrive surveys,
  With steadfast eye, the fell machine.

He mounts the platform—takes his stand
  Before the fatal block, and kneels
In preparation—but his hand
  A soft warm touch that moment feels.

His eyes glance downward, and a tear—
  The last tear they shall ever shed—
Falls as he utters, " *Thou* still here!"
  Upon his faithful servant's head.

Yes—she is there! that hellish shout,
   That deadly stroke, she hears them plain,
And from the headless trunk starts out,
   Even over her, the bloody rain.

And she beholds where they have cast
   (Uncoffined, bleeding yet, and warm,
His shallow grave filled up in haste
   Without a prayer) that mangled form.

But where is all the tumult now?
   That horrid engine, blood-imbrued,
That corse yet quivering with the blow,
   That gazing, shouting multitude?

All passed away—all vanished—gone—
   Even like a vision seen in sleep!
And in its stead, lies all alone
   A dog beside a fresh turned heap.

Old faithful Nina! there lies she,
   Her cold head on the cold earth pressed,
As it was wont so lovingly
   To lie upon her master's breast.

And there she stayed the livelong day,
   Mute, motionless, her sad watch keeping:
A stranger who had passed that way,
   Would have believed her dead or sleeping.

But if a step approached the grave,
   Her eye looked up with jealous care
Imploringly, as if to crave
   That no rude foot should trample there.

That night she came not as of late
  To her old charitable home:
The next day's sun arose and set,
  Night fell—and still she failed to come.

Then the third day her pitying host
  Went kindly forth to seek his guest,
And found her at her mournful post
  Stretched quietly, as if at rest.

Yet she was not asleep nor dead;
  And when her master's friend she saw,
The poor old creature raised her head,
  And moaned, and moved one feeble paw,

But stirred not thence—and all in vain
  He called, caressed her, would have led—
Tried threats—then coaxing words again—
  Brought food—she turned away her head.

So with kind violence at last
  He bore her home: with gentle care
In her old shelter tied her fast,
  Placed food beside, and left her there.

But ere the hour of rest, again
  He visited the captive's shed,
And there the cord lay, gnawed in twain—
  The food untasted—she was fled.

And, vexed, he cried, "Perverse old creature!
  Well, let her go, I've done my best."
But there was something in his nature,
  A feeling would not let him rest.

So, with the early light, once more
  Towards the burial-ground went he;
And there he found her as before,
  But not as then stretched quietly;

For she had worked the long night through,
  In the strong impulse of despair,
Down, down into the grave—and now,
  Panting and weak, still laboured there.

But death's cold stiffening frost benumbs
  Her limbs, and clouds her heavy eye—
And hark! her feeble moan becomes
  A shriek of human agony.

As if before her task was over,
  She feared to die in her despair—
But see! those last faint strokes uncover
  A straggling lock of thin grey hair.

One struggle! one convulsive start!
  And there the face belovèd lies—
Now be at peace, thou faithful heart!
  She licks the livid lips, and dies.

—o—

"SUFFICIENT UNTO THE DAY IS THE EVIL THEREOF."

OH! by that gracious rule
  Were we but wise to steer
On the wide sea of Thought,
What moments, trouble-fraught,
  Were spared us here!

But we, perverse and blind,
    As covetous of pain,
Not only seek for more
Yet hidden, but live o'er
    The past again.

This life is callèd brief—
    Man on the earth but crawls
His threescore years and ten—
At best fourscore—and then
    The ripe fruit falls.

Yet, betwixt birth and death,
    Were but the life of man
By his *thoughts* measured,
To what an age would spread
    That little span!

There are, who're born and die,
    Eat, sleep, walk, rest between—
Talk—*act* by clockwork too,
So pass, in order due,
    Over the scene.

With whom the past *is past*,
    The future, *nothing yet;*
And so, from day to day
They breathe, till called to pay
    The last great debt.

Their life, in truth, *is* brief;
    A speck—a point of time,
Whether in good old age
Endeth their pilgrimage,
    Or in its prime.

"Sufficient unto the day is the evil thereof."

But other some there are
    (I call them not more wise),
In whom the restless mind
Still lingereth behind,
    Or forward flies.

With *these*, things pass away;
    But past things are not dead;
In the heart's treasury,
Deep-hidden, dead they lie,
    Unwitherèd.

And there the soul retires,
    From the dull things that are,
To mingle oft and long
With the time-hallowed throng
    Of those that were.

Then into life start out
    The scenes long vanishèd;
Then we behold again
The forms that long have lain
    Among the dead.

We seek their grasp of love,
    We meet their beaming eye;
We speak—the vision's flown,
Dissolving with its own
    Intensity.

Years rapidly shift on,
    Like clouds athwart the sky,
And lo! sad watch we keep,
When, in perturbèd sleep,
    The sick doth lie.

"Sufficient unto the day is the evil thereof."

We gaze on some pale face,
    Shown by the dim watch-light;
Shuddering we gaze, and pray,
And weep, and wish away
    The long, long night.

And yet minutest things,
    That mark time's tedious tread,
Are on the feverish brain,
With self-protracting pain,
    Deep minuted :—

The drops with trembling hand,
    Love-steadied, pourèd out—
The draught replenishèd—
The label oft re-read
    With nervous doubt—

The watch that ticks so loud—
    The winding it for one
Whose hand lies powerless—
And then the fearful guess,—
    " Ere *this* hath run . . . ."

The shutter half unclosed
    As the night wears away,
Ere the last stars are set—
Pale stars !—that linger yet
    Till perfect day—

The morn, so oft invoked,
    That bringeth no relief,
From which, with sickening sight,
We turn, as if its light
    But mocked our grief.

"Sufficient unto the day is the evil thereof."

Oh, never after-dawn
    For us the east shall streak,
But we shall see again,
With the same thoughts as then,
    That pale daybreak!

The desolate awakening,
    When first we feel alone!
"Dread memories" are these!—
Yet who, for heartless ease,
    Would exchange one?

These are the soul's hid wealth—
    Relics embalmed with tears.
Or, if her curious eye
Searcheth futurity—
    The depth of years;

There, from the deck of youth,
    Enchanted land she sees;
Blue skies and sun-bright bowers
Reflected, and tall towers,
    On glassy seas.

But heavy clouds collect
    Over that bright blue sky;
And rough winds rend the trees,
And lash those glassy seas
    To billows high!

And then, the last thing seen
    By that dim light may be,
With helm and rudder lost,
A lone wreck, tempest-tost,
    On the dark sea!

Thus doth the soul extend
    Her brief existence *here*,
Thus multiplieth she—
Yea, to infinity—
    The short career.

Presumptuous and unwise!
    As if the present sum
Were little of life's woe!
Why seeketh she to know
    Ills yet to come?

Look up, look up, my soul,
    To loftier mysteries;
Trust in His word to thee,
Who saith, "All tears shall be
    Wiped from all eyes."

And when thou turnest back
    (Oh, what can chain thee *here?*),
Seek out the isles of light
On "memory's waste" yet bright;
    Or if too near

To desolate plains they lie,
    All dark with guilt and tears,
Still, still retrace the past,
Till thou alight at last
    On life's first years.

There not a passing cloud
    Obscures the sunny scene;
No blight on the young tree;
No thought of what *may be*,
    Or what *hath been*.

There all is Hope—*not* hope—
    For all things are possest.
No—bliss without alloy,
And innocence and joy,
    In the young breast.

And all-confiding love,
    And holy ignorance—
Thrice blessed veil!—soon torn
From eyes foredoomed to mourn
    For man's offence.

Oh, thither, weary spirit!
    Flee from this world defiled.
How oft, heart-sick and sore,
I've wished I were once more
    A little child!

―――*o*―――

FAREWELL TO MY FRIENDS.

OH, wear no mourning weeds for me,
    When I am laid i' the ground!
Oh, shed no tears for one whose sleep
    Will then be sweet and sound!

Only, my friends, do this for me,—
    Pluck many a pale primrose,
And strew them on my shroud, before
    The coffin-lid they close.

And lay the heart's-ease on my breast—
  Meet emblem there 'twill be—
And gently place in my cold hand
  A sprig of rosemary.

And by the buried bones of those
  Whom living I loved best,
See me at last laid quietly,
  Then leave me to my rest.

And when the church-bell tolls for me
  Its last, long, hollow knell,
As the deep murmur dies away,
  Bid me a kind farewell.

And, stay!—Methinks there's something yet
  I'd fain request of thee—
Something I'd bid ye comfort, keep,
  Or love, for love of me.

My nurse!—Oh, she will only wait
  Till I am fast asleep,
Then close beside me, stealthily,
  To her own pillow creep.

My dog!—Poor fellow! let him not
  Know hunger, hardship, wrong:
But he is old and feeble too—
  He will not miss me long.

My dwelling!—That will pass away
  To those, when I am gone,
Will raze the lowly edifice
  To its foundation-stone.

My flowers!—That in deep loneliness
    Have been as friends to me.
My garden!—That, let run to waste,
    A common field will be.

My picture!—That's already yours—
    Resemblance true, ye say:
Oh, true indeed! A thing of dust,
    That vanisheth away!

My harp!—But that's a fairy gift
    I can bequeath to none.
Unearthly hands will take it back
    When the last strain is done.

So, then, I've nothing more to ask,
    And little left to give;
And yet I know in your kind hearts
    My memory will live.

And so farewell, my dear good friends!
    And farewell, world, to thee!
I part with some in love—with all
    In peace and charity.

TO A DYING INFANT.

SLEEP, little Baby! sleep!
    Not in thy cradle bed,
Not on thy mother's breast
Henceforth shall be thy rest,
    But with the quiet dead.

To a Dying Infant.

Yes, with the quiet dead,
    Baby! thy rest shall be—
Oh! many a weary wight,
Weary of life and light,
    Would fain lie down with thee!

Flee, little tender nursling!
    Flee to thy grassy nest—
There the first flowers shall blow,
The first pure flake of snow
    Shall fall upon thy breast

Peace! peace! the little bosom
    Labours with shortening breath.
Peace! peace! that tremulous sigh
Speaks his departure nigh—
    Those are the damps of Death.

I've seen thee in thy beauty,
    A thing all health and glee;
But never then wert thou
So beautiful, as now,
    Baby! thou seem'st to me.

Thine upturned eyes glazed over
    Like harebells wet with dew—
Already veiled and hid
By the convulsèd lid,
    Their pupils darkly blue.

Thy little mouth half open,
    The soft lip quivering,
As if, like summer air,
Ruffling the rose leaves, there
    Thy soul were fluttering.

To a Dying Infant.

Mount up, immortal essence!
    Young spirit! hence—depart!
And is *this* Death? Dread thing!
If such thy visiting,
    How beautiful thou art!

Oh! I could gaze for ever
    Upon that waxen face,
So passionless! so pure!
The little shrine was sure
    An angel's dwelling-place.

Thou weepest, childless mother!
    Ay, weep—'twill ease thine heart;
He was thy first-born son—
Thy first, thine only one;
    'Tis hard from him to part.

'Tis hard to lay thy darling
    Deep in the damp cold earth,
His empty crib to see,
His silent nursery,
    Late ringing with his mirth.

To meet again in slumber
    His small mouth's rosy kiss,
Then—wakened with a start
By thine own throbbing heart—
    His twining arms to miss.

And then to lie and weep,
    And think the livelong night—
Feeding thine own distress
With accurate greediness—
    Of every past delight;

To a Dying Infant.

Of all his winning ways,
    His pretty, playful smiles,
His joy at sight of thee,
His tricks, his mimickry,
    And all his little wiles.

Oh! these are recollections
    Round mothers' hearts that cling!
That mingle with the tears
And smiles of after years,
    With oft awakening.

But thou wilt then, fond mother,
    In after years look back—
Time brings such wondrous easing—
With sadness not unpleasing,
    Even on this gloomy track.

Thou'lt say, "My first-born blessing!
    It almost broke my heart,
When thou wert forced to go;
And yet for thee, I know,
    'Twas better to depart.

"God took thee in His mercy,
    A lamb untasked—untried—
He fought the fight for thee,
He won the victory—
    And thou art sanctified.

"I look around, and see
    The evil ways of men,
And oh, beloved child!
I'm more than reconciled
    To thy departure then.

"The little arms that clasped me,
 The innocent lips that prest—
Would they have been as pure
Till now, as when of yore
 I lulled thee on my breast?

"Now, like a dewdrop shrined
 Within a crystal stone,
Thou'rt safe in heaven, my dove!
Safe with the Source of love,
 The everlasting One!

"And when the hour arrives,
 From flesh that sets me free,
Thy spirit may await
The first at heaven's gate,
 To meet and welcome me."

—o—

MY OLD DOG AND I.

"NAY, not to-day, my good old fellow—
 We can't go out to-day;
Look! this long sheet must be crammed over—
All this—with words as thick as clover,
 To go by post away!"

"And *must* it go to-day?"—"Yes, sir!
 Methinks you heard me say it—
It's of great consequence—the Press
Would wait in infinite distress
 Should anything delay it."

My Old Dog and I.

"But, Mistress! what a morning—see—
    For winter!"—"Well, what then?"
"Only methought the warm sunshine
Would comfort these old limbs of mine."
    "Pshaw! there I've dropt my pen,

"And made a blot—it's all your fault,
    You teasing thing! I wish——"
"What, mistress? If 'twere mine to grant,
Your heart should not know wish or want
    Deferred a minute."—"Pish!

"Old cunning fox! but that won't do;
    And pray, sir! after all,
Why can't you by yourself stroll down,
As you used often, to the town,
    And make a morning call?"

"Because those friends of mine are gone—
    Their like won't come again—
Who used to save the greasy platters,
And other little savoury matters,
    For my refreshment then.

"Besides—I hate to walk alone—
    My eyes grow very dim;
I'm hard of hearing, too—a fly
Might knock me down, so weak am I
    In every trembling limb.

"And now vile curs make sport of me—
    Vile creatures: but last week
Pounced on my back an old fat hen,
And pecked me, till I howled again
    At every spiteful tweak."

"But, Mister Ranger! who attacked
  Her harmless chickens, pray?"
"Well—if I did—'twas all in fun—
Mere frolic; that I throttled *one*,
  No living soul can say."

"No fault of yours?—D'ye mind, old friend!
  That *Goose*—that *Turkey*, too?"
"Why, ay—but then they were your cousin's,
And he had plenty more—whole dozens!
  I smote the fowls for you."

"Was it for my sake, yesterday,
  You flew at the calf's throat?"
"Yes; because Lizzy fed the beast,
Forsooth—I thought she did, at least—
  From your choice butterboat."

"Oh, rare!—and, when you stole the ham,
  No doubt, 'twas all pure zeal
For *my* wronged interest made you do it."
"Ah, Mistress! sorely did I rue it,
  That sinful savoury meal!

"How sick I was!—what stuff I took—
  What solemn vows did utter,
Never to touch fish, flesh, or fowl,
Forbidden thing——" "And so you stole,
  Next time, a pound of butter.—

"Then you're so rude!—when people call,
  And your good leave outstay,
You go and stick yourself before 'em
Bolt upright—outraging decorum—
  To beg they'll go away.

" 'Tis true, *they* don't quite comprehend
    Your meaning—but *I* do;
And when they call you 'civil creature!'
And praise your sweet obliging nature—
    Ranger!—I blush for you——"

"Why, mistress! sure I've heard you say,
    'Good heavens!—I'm almost dead—
Those people stayed so!'"—"Come, no sneering—
When they were fairly out of hearing,
    No matter what I said.

"You're such a jealous, envious thing!
    You've ousted the poor cat;
And now, forsooth! if I but throw
The guinea-fowls a crumb or so,
    You take offence at that;

"And growl, and snarl, and snap at them—
    Would kill them, if you durst.
It really shocks me, I must own,
To think of late your temper's grown
    So crabbed and so curst."

"Bear with me, Mistress!—I was not
    Always so curst a creature—
Perhaps old age, that on me gains
So fast, with all its aches and pains,
    Has something changed my nature,

"But not my heart. I've served you now
    These eighteen years, wellnigh—
Borne all your humours—for *you*, too,
Mine honoured Mistress, have a few—
    You'll own, right lovingly;

" Shared all your good and evil days—
        Much evil have we known!—
Loved those you loved, and mourned them too,
And missed them long, as well as you;
        And now we're left alone.

" I do my best—my very best—
        To please and cheer you still;
Though weak and weaker every hour
Becomes your poor old servant's power
        To prove his loving will.

" But yet a little longer, pray,
        Bear with me, Mistress mine!
It won't be long—and when I'm dead——"
" Thou'lt leave behind no craftier head
        Than that old pate of thine.

" Serpent of guile! and thus it is
        You always wind about,
And whatsoever thing I'm doing,
Though leaving it were certain ruin,
        You're sure to get me out.

" There! there!—I've shut the blotting-book,
        Bid Honour bring my cloak,
She understands your bark as well
As if I called, or rang the bell—
        Peace, peace, old fool! you'll choke.

" Well!—I'm just ready—get you gone—
        But now—d'ye mind me, Ranger!
Don't bark at everything we meet,
And make a riot in the street,
        And get yourself in danger.

" And don't attack the baker's dog—
    Nor snap and snarl at Beau—
Nor hunt the cats, nor rouse again
The wrath of your old friend the Hen—— "
" Trust me for that—No, no !

" Hang her, old toad !—I'm no match now
    For that audacious creature ;
I'd snap her head off, if I could—
Old Hens are pretty picking, stewed—
    Do, Mistress !—buy and eat her."

―—o―—

RANGER'S GRAVE.

March 1825.

HE'S dead and gone !—he's dead and gone !
    And the lime-tree branches wave,
  And the daisy blows,
  And the green grass grows
    Upon his grave.

He's dead and gone !—he's dead and gone !
    And he sleeps by the flowering lime,
  Where he loved to lie,
  When the sun was high,
    In summer time.

We've laid him there, for I could not bear
    His poor old bones to hide

In some dark hole,
Where rat and mole
  And blindworms bide.

We've laid him there, where the blessed air
  Disports with the lovely light,
    And raineth showers
    Of those sweet flowers
      So silver white;

Where the blackbird sings, and the wild-bee's wings
  Make music all day long,
    And the cricket at night—
    A dusky sprite!—
      Takes up the song.

He loved to lie where his wakeful eye
  Could keep me still in sight,
    Whence a word or a sign,
    Or a look of mine,
      Brought him like light.

Nor word, nor sign, nor look of mine,
  From under the lime-tree bough,
    With bark and bound,
    And frolic round,
      Shall bring him now.

But he taketh his rest, where he lovèd best
  In the days of his life to be,
    And that place will not
    Be a common spot
      Of earth to me.

THE MARINER'S HYMN.

LAUNCH thy bark, Mariner!
    Christian, God speed thee!
Let loose the rudder-bands—
    Good angels lead thee!
Set thy sails warily,
    Tempests will come;
Steer thy course steadily,
    Christian, steer home!

Look to the weather-bow,
    Breakers are round thee;
Let fall the plummet now,
    Shallows may ground thee.
Reef in the foresail, there!
    Hold the helm fast!
So—let the vessel wear—
    There swept the blast.

"What of the night, watchman?
    What of the night?"
"Cloudy—all quiet—
    No land yet—all's right!"
Be wakeful, be vigilant—
    Danger may be
At an hour when all seemeth
    Securest to thee.

How! gains the leak so fast?
    Clear out the hold—
Hoist up thy merchandise,
    Heave out thy gold;—

There—let the ingots go—
   Now the ship rights;
Hurrah! the harbour's near—
   Lo, the red lights!

Slacken not sail yet
   At inlet or island;.
Straight for the beacon steer,
   Straight for the high land;
Crowd all thy canvass on,
   Cut through the foam—
Christian! cast anchor now—
   Heaven is thy home!

—o—

SONNET,

WRITTEN ON READING TASSO'S LIFE.

REST, weary spirit, from thy labours past—
   Thy doubts, thy wrongs, thy painful wanderings o'er,
Through troubled seas, thy bark has reached at last,
   The quiet haven of a friendly shore.
Yes—"after death"—around thy pallid brow
   They wreathed the laurel, long, too long denied,
For which, in all the ambitious ardent glow
   Of conscious worth, thy once proud spirit sighed.
But when the mortal scene was closing fast
   Around thee, Tasso! on that proferred crown
What cold, contemptuous glances didst thou cast!
   Earth could no longer chain the spirit down,
That, fixing on a heavenly crown its trust,
Bequeathed the earthly to its mouldering dust.

THE BROKEN BRIDGE.

IT was a lovely autumn morn,
    So indistinctly bright,
So many-hued, so misty, clear,
So blent the glittering atmosphere,
    A web of opal light!

The morning mist, from the hill-top,
    Sailed off—a silvery flake—
But still in the under vale it lay,
Where the trees peered out like islands grey,
Seen dimly, at the dawn of day,
    On a waveless pearly lake.

And again, when we reached the woody rise
    That Boldre church doth crown,
The filmy shroud was wafted by,
And, rejoicing in his victory,
    The dazzling sun looked down.

We reached the church, a two-mile walk,
    Just as the bell begun;
Only the clerk was stationed there,
And one old man with silver hair,
    Who warmed him in the sun.

A gravestone for his seat—one hand
    On his old staff leant he;
The other fondly dallièd
With the bright curls of a young head
    That nestled on his knee.

The child looked up in the old man's face,
    Looked up and laughed the while—
Methought 'twas a beautiful sight to see
The reflected light of its innocent glee—
Like a sunbeam on a withered tree—
    In the old man's quiet smile.

That simple group well harmonised
    With the surrounding scene—
The old grey church, with its shadows deep,
Where the dead seemed hushed in sounder sleep;
And all beyond, where the sun shone bright,
Touching the tombstones with golden light,
    And the graves with emerald green.

And a redbreast from the elms hard by
    His joyous matins sung;
That music wild contrasted well
With the measured sound of the old church-bell,
    In its low square tower that swung.

I looked, and listened, and listened still,
    But word spake never a one;
And I started like one awakenèd
From a trance, when my young companion said,
    "Let's walk till the bell has done."

So we turned away by the shady path
    That winds down the pleasant hill—
Leaving the churchyard to the right
High up, it brought us soon in sight
Of the clear stream, so splarkling bright,
    That turns old Hayward mill.

The Broken Bridge.

A lovely scene! but not therefore
    Young Edmund's choice, I doubt;
No, rather that with barbèd snare
For sport he oft inveigled there
    The perch and speckled trout.

Stopt was the busy mill-wheel now,
    Snareless the rippling brook,
And up the finny people leapt,
As if they knew that danger slept—
And Edmund! he had wellnigh wept
    For lack of line and hook.

"Look, what a fish! the same, I'll swear,
    That I hooked yesterday—
He's a foot long from head to tail—
The fellow tugged like any whale,
And broke my line—it's very true,
Though you laugh, miss! you always do
    At everything I say."

"Nay, gentle coz! I did but smile—
    But—*was* he a foot long?"
"Ay, more, a foot and half—near two—
There, there, there's no convincing *you*,
One might as well to an old shoe
    Go whistle an old song."

"Gramercy, coz! I only asked,
    In admiration strong."
"Ay, but you look at one so queer—
Oh! that I had my tackle here,
You should soon see—well, never fear,
    I'll have him yet ere long."

"Ay, doubtless—but, dear Edmund! now
  Be murderous thoughts far hence;
This is a day of peace and rest,
And should diffuse in every breast
  Its holy influence."

Such desultory chat we held,
  Still idly sauntering on
Towards the old crazy bridge, that led
Across the stream by the mill-head—
  "Heyday!" said I, "'tis gone!"

And gone it was, but planks and piles
  Lay there, a fresh-brought load,
And, till a better bridge was made,
Flat stones across the brook were laid,
  So one might pass dryshod.

One with firm foot and steady eye,
  Dryshod might pass the brook—
But now, upon the further side,
A woman and a child we spied;
And those slippery stones the woman eyed
  With vexed and angry look.

And the child stood there—a pretty boy,
  Some seven years old looked he,
Limber and lithe as a little fawn,
And I marvelled much that he sprang not on
  With a boy's activity.

But his head hung down like a dew-bent flower,
  And he stood there helplessly;

The Broken Bridge.

And the woman—an old ill-favoured crone!—
Scowled at him, and said, in a sharp cross tone,
   " You're always a plague to me!"

" What ails you, my little man?" said I;
   " Such a light free thing as you
Should bound away, like a nimble deer,
From stone to stone, and be over here
   Before one could well count two."

The child looked up—to my dying day
   That look will haunt my mind.
The woman looked too, and she tuned her throat,
As she answered me, to a softer note,
   And says she, " The poor thing's blind.

" His father, who's dead, was my sister's son;
   Last week his mother died too.
He's but a weakly thing, you see,
Yet the parish has put him upon me,
   Who am but ill to do.

" And his mother made him more helpless still
   Than else he might have been;
For she nursed him up like a little lamb,
That in winter time has lost its dam;—
   Such love was never seen!

" To be sure he was her only one,
   A helpless thing, you see;
So she toiled and toiled to get him bread,
And to keep him neat, 'twas her pride, she said—
Well, 'tis a hard thing, now she's dead,
   To have him thrown on me.

"And now we shall be too late for church,
  For he can't get over, not he!
I thought the old bridge did well enough,
But they're always at some altering stuff,
  Hindering poor folks like we."

I looked about, but from my side
  Edmund was gone already,
And, with the child claspt carefully,
Across the stream back bounded he
  With firm foot, light and steady.

"And the woman," said I, "won't you help her too?
  Look, there she waits the while."
"Hang her, old cat! if I do," quoth he,
"To souse her into the midst 'twill be"—
  For my life I could not but smile.

So we left her to cross as best she might.
  And I turned to the sightless child;
His old white hat was wound about
With a rusty crape, and fair curls waved out
  On a brow divinely mild.

And the tears still swam in his large blue eyes,
  And hung on his sickly cheek—
Those eyes with their clouded vacancy,
That looked *towards*, but not *at* me,
Yet spoke to my heart more touchingly
  Than the brightest could ever speak.

I took his little hand in mine—
  'Twas a delicate small hand—

And the poor thing soon crept close to me,
With a timid familiarity,
No heart could e'er withstand.

By this time the woman had hobbled up.
" Ah, Goody! what, safe ashore ? "
Quoth Edmund—" I knew without help from me
You'd paddle across." Askance looked she,
But spake not a word; so in company
We moved on to church all four.

But I felt the child's hand, still held in mine,
With a shrinking dread compressed;
"Do you love to go to church ?" I said.
" Yes;" and he hung down his little head,
" But I love the churchyard best."

" The churchyard, my pretty boy! And why?
Come tell me why, and how ? "
" Because—because—" and the poor thing
Sobbed out the words half whispering—
" 'Cause mammy is there now."

Feelings too deep for utterance
Shrilled me a moment's space;
At last—" My little friend," said I,
" She's gone to live with God on high,
In heaven, His dwelling-place.

" And if you're good, and pray to Him,
And tell the truth alway,
And bear all hardships patiently,
You'll go there too."—" But when ? " said he;
" Shall I go there to-day?"

"Nay, you must wait till God is pleased
    To call you to His rest."
"When will that be?" he asked again.
"Perhaps not yet, my child."—"Oh, then!
    I love the churchyard best."

And to the churchyard we were come,
    And close to the church door—
And the little hand I held in mine,
Still held, loath was I to resign ; .
And from that hour the face so mild,
And the soft voice of that orphan child,
    Have haunted me evermore.

―――o―――

SONNET.

WHAT if the tale was true, as some believe,
    That Tasso's love to Leonora gave?
Oh! happy Leonora, to receive
    Such fame-conferring vows from such a slave!
Darling of many hearts! Of short-lived fame
    The favoured minion! born in courts to shine!
Yet but for *him*, for *his* illustrious name,
    What deathless annals had recorded thine?
These are thy triumphs, Genius! flames that burn
    With brightening glory through the mists of time—
When earth-born spirits to the earth return,
    Thine mounting from thine ashes soars sublime;
And where *they* moulder, Contemplation's eye
With awful reverence dwells, when kings forgotten lie.

THE LADYE'S BRYDALLE.

"COME hither, come hither, my little foot-page,
    And beare to my gaye ladye
This ringe of the good red gowde, and be sure
    Rede well what she tellethe to thee.

"And take tent, little page, if my ladye's cheeke
    Be with watchinge and weepinge pale;
If her locks are unkempt, and her bonnie eyes redde;
    And come backe and telle me thye tale.

"And marke, little page, when thou showest the ringe,
    If she snatchethe it hastelye,
If the red blude mount up her slendere throate
    To her forehedde of ivorye.

"And take good heede, if, for gladnesse or griefe,
    So chaungethe mye ladye's cheere;
You shalle know bye her eyes, if their lichte laugh oute,
    Through the miste of a startinge teare,

"Like the summer sunne through a morninge cloude,
    There needeth no furthere tokenne,
That mye ladye brighte to her owne true knighte
    Hath keepit her faithe unbrokenne.

"Now ride, little page, for the sunne peeres oute
    Owre the rimme of the eastern heavenne,
And backe thou must bee with thy tidinges to mee
    Ere the shadowe falles far at evenne."

The Ladye's Brydalle.

Awaye and awaye! and he's farre on his waye,
    The little foot-page alreddye;
For he's backed on his lorde's own gallante graye,
    That steede so swift and steddye.

But the knighte stands there like a charmedde manne,
    Watchinge with eare and eye
The clatteringe speede of his noble steede,
    That swifte as the windes doth flye.

But the windes and the lichtninges are loitererres alle
    To the glaunce of a luver's mynde;
And Sir Alwynne, I trow, had thocht Bonnybelle slowe,
    Had her fleetnesse outstrippit the wynde.

Beseemed to him that the sunne once more
    Had stayedde his course that daye;
Never sicke manne longed for morninge licht,
    As Sir Alwynne for eveninge graye.

But the longeste daye must ende at laste,
    And the brighteste sunne must sette:
Where stayde Sir Alwynne at peepe of dawne,
    There at even he stayethe him yette.

And he spyethe at last——"Not soe, not soe;
    'Tis a small graye cloude, Sir Knighte,
That risethe up like a courser's hedde
    On that borderre of gowden licht."

"Bot harke! bot harke! for I heare it nowe;
    'Tis the comynge of Bonnybelle!"
"Not soe, Sir Knighte! from that rockye height,
    'Twas a clatteringe stone that felle."

The Ladye's Brydalle.

"That slothfulle boye!—but I'll thinke no more
  Of him and that lagginge jade to-daye."
"Righte, righte, Sir Knighte!"—"Nay, now by this lichte,
  Here comethe my page and my gallante graye!"

"Howe nowe, little page! ere thou lichteste downe,
  Speake but one worde out hastylye;
Little page, hast thou seen mye ladye luve?
  Hathe mye ladye keepit her faith with me?"

"I've scene thye ladye luve, Sir Knighte,
  And welle hathe she keepit her faithe with thee."
"Lichte downe, lichte downe, mye trustye page;
  A berrye browne barbe shall thy guerdon be.

"Telle on, telle on! Was mye ladye's cheeke
  Pale as the lilye, or rosye redde?
Did she put the ringe on her finger smalle?
  And what was the very firste worde she sedde?"

"Pale was thye ladye's cheeke, Sir Knighte;
  Blent with no streake of the rosye redde.
I put the ringe on her finger smalle:
  But there is no voice amongste the dedde."

*   *   *   *   *   *

There are torches hurryinge to and froe
  In Raeburne Towerre to-nighte,
And the chapelle dothe glowe with lampes alsoe,
  As if for a brydalle ryte.

The Ladye's Brydalle.

But where is the bryde? and the brydegroome where?
    And where is the holye prieste?
And where are the guestes that shoulde biddenne be,
    To partake of the marriage feast?

The bryde from her chamberre descendethe slowe,
    And the brydegroome her hande hath ta'en,
And the guestes are mette, and the holy prieste
    Precedethe the marriage traine.

The bryde is the fayre Maude Winstanlye,
    And Dethe her sterne brydegroome;
And her father followes his onlye childe
    To her mothere's yawninge tombe.

An agedde manne! and a wofulle manne!
    And a heavye moane makes he:
"Mye childe! mye childe! mine onlye childe!
    Would God I had dyedde for thee!"

An agedde manne, those white haires telle,
    And that bendedde backe and knee;
Yette a stalwart knighte at Tewkesburye fighte
    Was Sir Archibalde Winstanlye.

'Tis a movinge thinge to see the teares
    Wrunge oute frae an agedde eye,
Seldome and slowe, like the scantye droppes
    Of a fountaine that's neere a-drye.

'Tis a sorrye sighte to see graye haires
    Brocht downe to the grave with sorrowe!
Youth lukes through the cloude of the presente daye
    For a goldenne gleame to-morrowe.

The Ladye's Brydalle.

Bot the palsyede hedde, and the feeble knees,
  Berefte of earthlye staye! . . . .
God help thee nowe, olde Winstanlye!
  Gude Christians for thee praye!—

Bot manye a voice in that burialle traine
  Breathes gloomilye aparte,
"Thou hadst not been childelesse nowe, olde manne,
  Bot for thine owne harde hearte!"

And manye a mayde, who strewethe floweres
  Afore the Ladye's biere,
Weepes oute, "Thou hadst not dyede, sweete Maude,
  If Alwynne had beene heere!"

* * * * * *

What solemne chaunte ascendeth slowe?
  What voices peale the straine?
The Monkes of St Switholm's Abbaye neare
  Have mette the funeralle traine.

They hold their landes, full many a roode,
  From the Knightes of Raeburne Towerre;
And everre when Dethe doth claime his preye
  From within that lordlye bowerre,

Then come the holye Fatheris forthe,
  The shrowdedde corse to meete,
And see it laide in hallowde grave,
  With requiem sadde and sweete.

And nowe they turne, and leade the waye
  To that laste home so nigh,
Where alle the race of Winstanlye
  In dust and darknesse lye.

The holye altarre blazethe brighte
  With waxenne taperres high;
Elsewhere, in dimme and doubtfulle lycht
  Doth alle the chapelle lye.

Huge undefinedde shadowes falle
  From pillare and from tombe;
And manye a grimme old monumente
  Lookes ghastelye through the gloome.

And manye a rustye shirt of maile
  The eye maye scantlye trace;
And crestedde helmette, blacke and barred,
  That grinnes with sterne grimace.

Bannerre and scutcheon from the walles
  Wave in the cald nighte aire;
Gleames oute their gorgeous heraldrye
  In the enteringe torches' glare.

For nowe the mourninge companye,
  Beneathe that archedde doore,
Beare in the lovelye, lifelesse claye,
  Shall passe thereoute no more.

And up the soundinge aisle ye stille
  Their solemne chaunte may heare;
Tille 'neath that blazonned catafalque
  They gentlye reste the biere:

The Ladye's Brydalle.

Then ceasethe everye sounde of life;
  So deepe that awfulle hushe,
Ye heare from yon freshe opennedde vaulte
  The hollowe deathe-winde rushe.

Backe from the biere the mournerres alle
  Retire a little space;
Alle bot that olde bereavedde manne,
  Who takethe there his place

Beside the dedde:—but none may see
  The workinges of his mynde;
So lowe upon that sunkenne breste
  Is that graye hedde declinede.

* * * * * *

The masse is saide, they raise the dedde,
  The palle is flunge aside;
And soone that coffinned lovelyenesse
  The darksome pit shalle hide.

It gapeth close at hande.—Deep downe
  Ye maye the coffinnes see,
By the lampe's dull glare, freshe kindledde there,
  Of many a Winstanlye.

And the gildedde nails on one looke brighte,
  And the velvette of cramoisie;
She hathe not laine there a calenderre yeere,
  The last Dame Winstanlye.

The Ladye's Brydalle.

"There's roome for thee heere, oh daughter deere!"
   Methinkes I heare her saye—
"There's roome for thee, Maude Winstanlye;
   Come downe—make no delaye!"

And, from the vaulte, two grimlye armes
   Upraised, demaunde the dedde! . . .
Hark! hark! 'tis the tramp of a rushinge steede!
   'Tis the clanke of an armedde tredde!

There's an armedde hedde at the chapelle doore;
   And in armoure all bedighte
In coal-black steele, from hedde to heele,
   In steppes an armedde Knighte!

And upp the aisle, with heavye tredde,
   Alone advauncethe he;
To barre his waye, dothe none essaye
   Of the funeralle companye.

And never a voice amongste them all
   Dothe aske who he mote be;
Nor why his armedde steppe disturbes
   That sadde solemnitye.

Yette manye an eye, with fixedde stare,
   Dothe sternelye on him frown;
Bot none may trace the straunger's face—
   He weares his vizorre downe.

He speakes no worde, but waves his hande,
   And straighte theye alle obeye;
And everye soule that standethe there,
   Falles backe to make him waye.

The Ladye's Brydalle.

He passethe on—no hande dothe stirre;
   His steppe the onlye sounde;
He passethe on, and signes them sette
   The coffinne on the grounde.

A momente gazinge down thereonne,
   With foldedde armes dothe staye;
Then stoopinge, with one mightye wrench
   He teares the lidde awaye.

Then risethe a confusedde sounde,
   And some half forwarde starte,
And murmurre "sacriledge!" And some
   Beare hastilye aparte

The agedde Knighte, at that straunge sighte
   Whose consciousnesse hathe fledde—
Bot signe nor sounde disturbethe him
   Who gazethe on the dedde.

And seemethe sune, as that faire face
   Dothe alle exposedde lye,
As if its holye calme o'erspredde
   The frowninge faces bye.

And nowe beside the Virginne corse
   Downe kneeles the straunger Knighte,
And backe his vizorrede helme he throwes,
   Bot not in openne sight;

For to the pale, colde clammye face,
   His owne he stoopethe lowe,
And kissethe firste the bludelesse cheeke,
   And then the marble browe.

Then, to the dedde lippes gluede, so long
    The livinge lippes do staye,
As if in that sad silente kisse
    The soule had paste awaye.

Bot suddenne, from that mortal trance,
    As with a desperate straine,
Up! up! he springes—his armoure ringes—
    His vizorre's downe againe.

With many a flouerre, her weepinge maydes
    The Layde's shroude have dressed;
And one white rose is in the faulde
    That veiles her whiterre breste.

One gowdenne ringlette on her browe,
    Escapedde forth, dothe straye;
So on a wreathe of driftedde snowe
    The wintrye sunbeames playe.

The mailedde hande hath ta'en the rose
    From offe that breste so fayre;
The faulchion's edge, from that pale hedde,
    Hath shorne the gowden haire.

One heavye sigh!—the firste and last—
    One deepe and stifledde groane!
A few longe strides, a clange of hoofes,
    And the armedde straunger's gone!

TO MY BIRDIE.

HERE'S only you an' me, Birdie! here's only you an'
me!
An' there you sit, you humdrum fowl,
Sae mute an' mopish as an owl—
                Sour companie!

Sing me a little sang, Birdie! lilt up a little lay!
When folks are here, fu' fain are ye
To stun them with yere minstrelsie
                The lee-lang day;

An' now we're only twa, Birdie! an' now we're only
twa;
'Twere sure but kind an' cozie, Birdie!
To charm, wi' yere wee hurdy-gurdie,
                Dull care awa'.

Ye ken, when folks are paired, Birdie! ye ken, when folks
are paired,
Life's fair, an' foul, and freakish weather,
An' light an' lumbrin' loads, thegither
                Maun a' be shared;

An' shared wi' lovin' hearts, Birdie! wi' lovin' hearts an'
free;
Fu' fashious loads may weel be borne,
An' roughest roads to velvet turn,
                Trod cheerfully.

To My Birdie.

We've a' our cares an' crosses, Birdie! we've a' our cares an' crosses;
    But then to sulk an' sit sae glum—
    Hout, tout!—what guid o' that can come
                To mend ane's losses?

Ye're clipt in wiry fence, Birdie! ye're clipt in wiry fence;
    An' aiblins I, gin I mote gang
    Upo' a wish, wad be or lang
                Wi' frien's far hence:

But what's a wish, ye ken, Birdie! but what's a wish, ye ken?
    Nae cantrip naig, like hers of Fife,
    Wha darnit wi' the auld weird wife,
                Flood, fell, an' fen.

'Tis true, ye're furnished fair, Birdie! 'tis true, ye're furnished fair,
    Wi' a braw pair o' bonnie wings,
    Wad lift ye whar yon laverock sings
                High up i' th' air;

But then that wire's sae strang, Birdie! but then that wire's sae strang!
    An' I mysel', sae seemin' free,
    Nae wings have I to waften me
                Whar fain I'd gang.

An' say we'd baith our wills, Birdie! we'd each our wilfu' way:
    Whar laverocks hover, falcons fly;
    An' snares an' pitfa's aften lie
                Whar wishes stray.

An' ae thing weel I wot, Birdie! an' ae thing weel I wot—
There's Ane abune the highest sphere,
Wha cares for a' His creatures here,
        Marks every lot:

Wha guards the crownèd king, Birdie! wha guards the crownèd king,
An' taketh heed for sic as me—
Sae little worth—an' e'en for thee,
        Puir witless thing!

Sae now, let's baith cheer up, Birdie! an' sin' we're only twa—
Aff han'—let's ilk ane do our best,
To ding that crabbit, cankered pest,
        Dull care awa'!

TO MY OLD CANARY.

'TIS many a long year now, Birdie!
   Ay, sure—some seven years good,
Since I rhymed to you one day,
On a certain morn of May,
   In an idle, sing-song mood.

I remember it all as well, Birdie,
   The hour, and the place, and the mood,
As if time, since slipt away,
Were little more than a day,
   And yet is it seven years good!

To My Old Canary.

A great sum of life struck off, Birdie!
 And I feel it has told with me:
But you're looking as young and bright
As you did in that May morn's light,
 And you're singing more merrily.

For then you were moping and mute, Birdie,
 Though I begged, and you seemed to hear me,
That you'd tune up that little throat,
But you never vouchsafed a note,
 Not a single note to cheer me.

And your silence seemed very unkind;
 For in sooth, as I well remember,
Though Earth wore her best array
That beautiful month of May,
 My heart was as sad as December.

For then first I felt myself lonely,
 Quite, quite left alone upon earth;
Hid for ever the last loving face,
And even the old dog's place
 Forsaken beside the hearth.

And I, though a sickly creature,
 Might still live lingering on,
Like a trampled passion-flower,
Torn down from its bonny bower,
 When all I had clung to was gone.

I sat at my pleasant window,
 Where the myrtle and rose peeped in,
And without such a smile serene
Pervaded the quiet scene,
 That sorrow seemed almost a sin,

And I tried to rejoice with Nature,
  For my heart was not sullen, though sad;
But the cloud of my spirit lay
On all beautiful things that day,
  And I could not—I *could not* be glad.

So I bent again to the task
  That had dropt unperceived on my knee,
And my needle began to ply,
Busily, busily,
  As fast as fast could be.

Stitch after stitch I set,
  Mechanically true;
But the seeming gaze intent,
On that dull labour bent,
  Had little with thought to do.

And soon from the careless finger
  A crimson drop was drawn;
And next, from a source less near,
Another, as crystal clear,
  Dropt on the snowy lawn.

And my sight grew dim, and again
  My hands fell listlessly,
And the sound of my very breath,
In that stillness as deep as death,
  Was a distress to me.

"Oh! for a sound of life
  From a single living thing,"
I passionately cried—
And *thou* wert by my side,
  Birdie! and didst not sing.

Then 'twas that rhymed remonstrance—
  So famous!—I spake to thee,
Not surely less improving,
Than it was deeply moving,
  And its effect on me

Was wondrously relieving;
  For as my verse flowed on,
Sad thoughts it did beguile,
And for a little while
  My loneliness was gone.

And from that very moment,
  Birdie, I do opine,
There has been more in thee
Than common eyes can see,
  Or any eyes but mine.

'Tis not because thy music
  Is ceaseless now all day—
As many a deafened guest
Can ruefully attest—
  That thus of thee I say:

But that when night is round us,
  And every guest is gone,
And by the taper's beam,
Or fire-light's ruddier gleam,
  I'm sitting all alone,

Forth from thy gilded prison
  Soft silvery tones 'gin swell,
More sweet and tender far
Than tenderest warblings are
  Of love-lorn Philomel;

And thou the while fast perched,
    As if asleep—so still!
That tremulous undertone,
Liquidly gurgling on,
    Like a tiny, tinkling rill.

And when I watch thee closer,
    Small creature! with surprise,
Half doubtful, if from thee
That marvellous melody,
    I meet thy watchful eyes,

Those bright black eyes, so strangely,
    Methinks, that answer mine;
It surely seems to me,
Some spirit thou must be,
    Pent in that plumy shrine;

But whether spirit, fairy,
    Or mortal fowl thou art,
I thank thee, pretty creature,
My comforter, my teacher,
    I thank thee from my heart!

My comforter I call thee—
    For many a heavy hour,
Hath lightened of its sadness,
Nay, half attuned to gladness,
    Thy small pipe's witching power.

And often-time while listening,
    I've caught the infectious tone,
And murmured fitful words,
And struck a few faint chords,
    Wild music of my own,

Till to the realms of Cloudland,
    Freed Fancy winged her flight,
Far, far beneath her leaving
This world of sin and grieving:
    So, Birdie, with good right

My *Comforter* I call thee—
    My *Teacher* thou shouldst be;
For sure some lesson holy,
Of wisdom meek and lowly,
    May reason learn from thee.

Debarred from choicest blessings,
    Inferior good to prize,
Thou hymn'st the light of heaven,
Though not to thee 'tis given
    To soar into the skies.

Content thou art, and thankful,
    For some poor gathered weed,
Though nature's chartered right
In gardens of delight
    Gave thee to sport and feed.

Thou renderest good for evil:
    For sad captivity
Sweet music—all thy treasure.
Oh, Birdie! when I measure
    Philosophy with thee,

I feel how much I'm wanting,
    Though more is given to me—
That thou, poor soulless creature,
Mayst truly be the teacher
    Of proud humanity.

TO THE MEMORY OF ISABEL SOUTHEY.

'TIS ever thus—'tis ever thus, when Hope hath built a bower
Like that of Eden, wreathed about with every thornless flower,
To dwell therein securely, the self-deceiver's trust,
A whirlwind from the desert comes, and "all is in the dust."

'Tis ever thus—'tis ever thus, that when the poor heart clings,
With all its finest tendrils, with all its flexile rings,
That goodly thing it cleaveth to, so fondly and so fast,
Is struck to earth by lightning, or shattered by the blast.

'Tis ever thus—'tis ever thus, with beams of mortal bliss,
With looks too bright and beautiful for such a world as this;
One moment round about us their "angel* lightnings" play,
Then down the veil of darkness drops, and all hath past away.

'Tis ever thus—'tis ever thus, with sounds too sweet for earth—
Seraphic sounds, that float away, borne heavenward, in their birth:
The golden shell is broken, the silver chord is mute,
The sweet bells all are silent, and hushed the lovely lute.

* "Il lampeggiar del angelico riso."

'Tis ever thus—'tis ever thus, with all that's best below;
The dearest, noblest, loveliest, are always first to go—
The bird that sings the sweetest, the pine that crowns the rock,
The glory of the garden, the flower of the flock.

'Tis ever thus—'tis ever thus, with creatures heavenly fair,
Too finely framed to 'bide the brunt more earthly natures bear;
A little while they dwell with us, blest ministers of love,
Then spread the wings we had not seen, and seek their home above.

---o---

SONNET.

TRAVELLER of Life! what plant of virtues rare
   Seeketh thy curious eye? 'Mongst earth's excess,
Will none but the exotic, Happiness,
Content thine eager longing? Fruitless care!
It groweth not beneath our clouded skies.
But when amongst the groves of Paradise
The soft winds wanton, haply they may bear,
   From thence to earth, some vagrant flower or leaf,
   Some fluttering petal, exquisite as brief
Its odorous beauty!—Oh, if to thy share
It fall, one blossom on thy path to find—
Quick! snatch it to thine heart, ere the rough wind
Despoil its freshness. It will fade e'en there;
Thou canst not quite exclude this cold world's nipping air.

THERE IS A TONGUE IN EVERY LEAF.

THERE is a tongue in every leaf,
    A voice in every rill!—
A voice that speaketh everywhere,
In flood and fire, through earth and air—
    A tongue that's never still!

'Tis the Great Spirit, wide diffused
    Through everything we see,
That with our spirits communeth
Of things mysterious—Life and Death—
    Time and Eternity.

I see him in the blazing sun,
    And in the thunder-cloud—
I hear him in the mighty roar,
That rusheth through the forest hoar
    When winds are piping loud.

I see him, hear him everywhere,
    In all things—Darkness, Light,
Silence, and Sound—but, most of all,
When slumber's dusky curtains fall
    At the dead hour of night.

I *feel* Him in the silent dews
    By grateful earth betrayed—
I *feel* Him in the gentle showers,
The soft south wind, the breath of flowers,
    The sunshine, and the shade.

And yet, ungrateful that I am!
   I've turned in sullen mood
From all these things—whereof He said,
When the great work was finishèd,
   That they were "Very good!"

My sadness on the fairest things
   Fell like unwholesome dew—
The darkness that encompassed me,
The gloom I felt so palpably,
   Mine own dark spirit threw.

Yet He was patient, slow to wrath,
   Though every day provoked
By selfish pining discontent,
Acceptance cold, or negligent,
   And promises revoked.

And still the same rich feast was spread
   For my insensate heart.
Not always so—I woke again
To join creation's rapturous strain—
   "O Lord! how good Thou art!"

The clouds drew up, the shadows fled,
   The glorious sun broke out—
And Love, and Hope, and Gratitude
Dispelled that miserable mood
   Of darkness and of doubt.

ON THE NEAR PROSPECT OF LEAVING HOME.—1818.

FAREWELL! farewell, beloved home!
　Haven of rest! a long farewell;
Where'er my weary footsteps roam,
　With thee shall faithful memory dwell.

They tell me other bowers will rise
　As fair in fancy's future view—
They little think what tender ties,
　Dear home! attach my heart to you.

Their happy childhood has not played,
　Like mine, beneath thy sheltering roof;
Thou hast not fostered, in thy shade,
　Their after-years of happier youth.

They cannot know, they have not proved
　The sympathies that make thee dear;
They have not here possessed and loved—
　They have not lost and sorrowed here.

In all around, they cannot see
　Relics of hopes, and joys o'ercast—
They have not learnt to live, like me,
　On recollections of the past;

To watch, as misers watch their gold,
　Tree, shrub, or flower—frail, precious trust!—
Planted and reared in days of old,
　By hands now mouldering in the dust;

To sanctify peculiar places,
　Associated in memory's glass,
With circumstances, times, and faces,
　That like a dream before me pass.

These are the feelings—*this* the band,
　Dear home! that knits my heart to thee;
No heart but mine can understand
　How strong that secret sympathy.

Therefore, of scenes more fair than thee,
　They kindly speak to soothe mine ear;
Yes—fairer other scenes may be,
　But never any half so dear.

—o—

AUTUMN FLOWERS.

THOSE few pale Autumn flowers!
　　How beautiful they are!
Than all that went before,
Than all the Summer store,
　　How lovelier far!

And why?—they are the *last*—
　　The last!—the last!—the last!—
Oh, by that little word,
How many thoughts are stirred!
　　That sister of the past!

Pale flowers!—pale perishing flowers!
  Ye're types of precious things;
Types of those bitter moments
That flit, like life's enjoyments,
  On rapid, rapid wings.

Last hours with parting dear ones—
  That time the fastest spends—
Last tears, in silence shed,
Last words, half utterèd,
  Last looks of dying friends!

Who but would fain compress
  A life into a day;
The last day spent with one,
Who, e'er the morrow's sun,
  Must leave us, and for aye?!

Oh, precious, precious moments!
  Pale flowers! ye're types of those—
The saddest, sweetest, dearest!
Because, like those, the nearest
  To an eternal close.

Pale flowers! pale perishing flowers!
  I woo your gentle breath;
I leave the summer rose
For younger, blither brows;
  Tell me of change and death!

TO DEATH.

COME not in terrors clad, to claim
    An unresisting prey:
Come like an evening shadow, Death!
    So stealthily, so silently!
And shut mine eyes, and steal my breath;
    Then willingly—oh! willingly,
With thee I'll go away.

What need to clutch with iron grasp
    What gentlest touch may take?
What need, with aspect dark, to scare,
    So awfully, so terribly,
The weary soul would hardly care,
    Called quietly, called tenderly,
From thy dread power to break?

'Tis not as when thou markest out
    The young, the blest, the gay,
The loved, the loving—they who dream
    So happily, so hopefully;
Then harsh thy kindest call may seem,
    And shrinkingly, reluctantly,
The summoned may obey.

But I have drunk enough of life—
    The cup assigned to me
Dashed with a little sweet at best,
    So scantily, so scantily—

To know full well that all the rest,
    More bitterly, more bitterly,
Drugged to the last will be.

And I may live to pain some heart
    That kindly cares for me—
To pain, but not to bless. O Death!
    Come quietly—come lovingly,
And shut mine eyes, and steal my breath;
    Then willingly—oh! willingly,
With thee I'll go away.

———o———

ONCE UPON A TIME.

SUNNY locks of brightest hue
    Once around my temples grew;—
Laugh not, lady, for 'tis true;
Laugh not, lady, for with thee
Time may deal despitefully;
Time, if long he lead thee here,
May subdue that mirthful cheer;
Round those laughing lips and eyes
Time may write sad histories;
Deep indent that even brow,
Change those locks, so sunny now,
To as dark and dull a shade,
As on mine his touch hath laid.
Lady! yes, these locks of mine
Clustered once with golden shine

Temples, neck, and shoulders round,
Richly gushing if unbound,
If from band and bodkin free,
Wellnigh downward to the knee.
Some there were took fond delight
Sporting with those tresses bright,
To enring with living gold
Fingers now beneath the mould,
Woe is me! grown icy cold.

One dear hand hath smoothed them too
Since they lost the sunny hue,
Since their bright abundance fell
Under the destroying spell—
One dear hand! the tenderest
Ever nurse child rocked to rest,
Ever wiped away its tears,
Even those of later years.
From a cheek untimely hollow,
Bitter drops that still may follow,
Where's the hand will wipe away?
Hers I kissed, ah! dismal day,
Pale as on the shroud it lay.
Then, methought, youth's latest gleam
Departed from me like a dream.
Still, though lost their sunny tone,
Glossy brown those tresses shone,
Here and there, in wave and ring,
Golden threads still glittering;
And, from band and bodkin free,
Still they flowed luxuriantly.

Careful days, and wakeful nights,
Early trenched on young delights.

Then of ills an endless train,
Wasting languor, wearying pain,
Feverish thought that racks the brain,
Crowding all on summer's prime,
Made me old before my time.
So a dull, unlovely hue
O'er the sunny tresses grew,
Thinned their rich abundance too.
Not a thread of golden light
In the sunshine glancing bright.

Now again a shining streak
'Gins the dusky cloud to break;
Here and there a glittering thread
Lights the ringlets, dark and dead—
Glittering light! but pale and cold—
Glittering thread! but not of gold.

Silent warning! silvery streak,
Not unheeded dost thou speak.
Not with feelings light and vain,
Not with fond regretful pain,
Look I on the token sent
To declare the day far spent.
Dark and troubled hath it been;
Sore misused! and yet between
Gracious gleams of peace and grace
Shining from a better place.

Brighten—brighten, blessed light!
Fast approach the shades of night;
When they quite enclose me round,
May my lamp be burning found!

THAT'S WHAT WE ARE.

CAREFUL and troubled about many things—
Alas! that it should be so with us still,
As in the days of Martha—I went forth,
Harassed and heartsick, with hot, aching brow,
Thought-fevered—haply to escape myself.

Beauteous that bright May morning—all about,
Sweet influences of earth, and air, and sky,
Harmoniously accordant. I alone—
The troubled spirit that had driven me forth—
In dissonance with that fair frame of things,
So blissfully serene. God had not yet
Let fall the weight of chastening, that makes dumb
The murmuring lip and stills the rebel heart,
Ending all earthly interests; and I called,
O heaven! that incomplete experience—Grief.
It would not do. The momentary sense
Of soft refreshing coolness passed away,
Back came the troublous thoughts, and all in vain
I strove with the tormentors: all in vain
Applied me with forced interest to peruse
Fair Nature's outspread volume: all in vain
Looked up admiring at the dappled clouds
And depths cerulean. Even as I gazed,
The film, the earthly film, obscured my vision,
And in a lower region, sore perplexed,
Again I wandered, and again shook off,
With vext impatience, the besetting cares,
And set me straight to gather, as I walked,
A field-flower nosegay. Plentiful the choice;

And in few moments, of all hues I held
A glowing handful. In few moments more
Where were they? Dropping as I went along
Unheeded on my path; and I was gone—
Wandering far off, in maze of thought perplext.

Despairingly I sought the social scene—
Sound—motion—action—interchange of *words*,
Scarcely of *mind*—rare privilege!
        We talked—
Oh! how we talked—discussed and solved all questions—
Religion, morals, manners, politics,
Physics and metaphysics, books and authors,
Fashion and dress, our neighbours and ourselves;
And ever as the senseless changes rang,
And I helped ring them, in my secret soul
Grew weariness, disgust, and self-contempt;
And, more disturbed in spirit, I resumed,
More cynically sad, my homeward way.

It led me through the Churchyard, and methought
There entering, as I let the iron gate
Swing to behind me, that the change was good,—
The unquiet living for the quiet dead.
And at that moment, from the old church-tower
A knell resounded—" Man to his long home
Drew near"—"The mourners went about the streets;"
And there, few paces onward, to the right,
Close by the pathway, lay an open grave—
Not of the humbler sort, shaped newly out,
Narrow and deep, in the dark mould; when filled
To be roofed over by the living sod,
And left for all adornment (and so best)
To Nature's reverential hand.

                                    The tomb
Made ready there for a new habitant
Was that of an old family: I knew it—
A very ancient altar-tomb, where Time
With his rough fretwork mocked the sculptor's art,
Feebly elaborate; heraldic shield
And mortuary emblems half effaced;
Deep sunken at one end, of many names
Graven with suitable inscription, each
Upon the shelving slab and sides, scarce now
Might any but an antiquarian eye
Make out a letter. Five-and-fifty years
The door of that dark dwelling had shut in
The last admitted sleeper. She, 'twas said,
Died of a broken heart—a widowed mother
Following her only child, by violent death
Cut off untimely—and the whisper went,
By his own hand. The tomb was ancient then,
When they two were interred; and they the first
For whom, within the memory of man,
It had been opened; and their names filled up—
With sharp-cut newness mocking the old stone—
The last remaining space. And so it seemed
The gathering was complete; the appointed number
Laid in the sleeping chamber, and sealed up
Inviolate, till the great reckoning day.
The few remaining of the name dispersed,
The family fortunes dwindled, till at last
They sank into decay, and out of sight,
And out of memory; till an aged man,
Passed by some parish very far away,
To die in ours—his legal settlement—
Claimed kindred with the long-forgotten race,
Its sole survivor, and in right thereof—

Of that affinity—to moulder with them
In the old family grave.
                    "A natural wish,"
Said the authorities; and "sure enough
He *was* of the old stock—the last descendant;
And it would cost no more to bury him
Under the old cracked tombstone, with its scutcheons,
Than in the common ground." So graciously
The boon was granted, and he died content.
And now the pauper's funeral had set forth,
And the bell tolled—not many strokes nor long—
Pauper's allowance;—he was coming home.
But while the train was yet a good way off—
The workhouse burial train—I stopt to look
Upon the scene before me; and methought—
Oh! that some gifted painter could behold
And give duration to that living picture,
So rich in moral and pictorial beauty,
If seen arightly by the spiritual eye,
As with the bodily organ!
                    The old tomb,
With its quaint tracery, gilded here and there
With sunlight glancing through the o'erarching lime,
Far flinging its cool shadow, flickering light;
Our grey-haired sexton, with his hard grey face—
A living tombstone—resting on his mattock
By the low portal; and just over right,
His back against the lime-tree, his thin hands
Locked in each other, hanging down before him
As with their own dead weight, a tall slim youth,
With hollow hectic cheek, and pale parched lip,
And labouring breath, and eye upon the ground
Fast rooted, as if taking measurement
Betime for his own grave. I stopt a moment,

M

Contemplating those thinkers—Youth and Age
Marked for the sickle, as it seemed, the *unripe*
To be first gathered.   Stepping forward, then,
Down to the house of death, with vague expectance
I sent a curious, not unshrinking gaze.
There lay the burning head and broken heart
Long, long at rest; and many *a thing* beside
That had been life—warm, sentient, busy life!—
Had hungered, thirsted, laughed, wept, hoped, and feared,
Hated and loved, enjoyed and agonised.
Where of all this was all I looked to see?—
The mass of crumbling coffins, some belike
Flattened and shapeless?   Even in this damp vault
With more completeness could the old Destroyer
Have done his darkling work?   Yet lo! I looked
Into a small square chamber, swept and clean,
Except that on one side, against the wall,
Lay a few fragments of dark rotten wood,
And a small heap of fine, rich, reddish earth
Was piled up in a corner.
                         " How is this ? "
In stupid wonderment I asked myself,
And dull of apprehension.   Turning then
To the old Sexton—" Tell me, friend," I said,
" Here *should be* many coffins—where are they ? "

He raised his eyes to mine with a strange look
And strangely meaning smile; and I repeated—
For not a word he spoke—my witless question.

Then with a deep distinctness he made answer,
Distinct and slow, looking to where I pointed,
Thence full into my face, and what he said
Thrilled through my very heart—" *That's what we are!* "

So I was answered. Sermons upon Death
I had heard many: Lectures by the score
Upon Life's vanities; but never words
Of mortal preacher to my heart struck home
With such convicting sense and suddenness,
As the plain-spoken homily, so brief,
Of that unlettered man.
     "That's what we are!"
Repeating after him, I murmured low,
In meek acknowledgment, and bowed the head
Profoundly reverential. A deep calm
Came over me, and to the inward eye
Vivid perception. Set against each other
I saw weighed out the things of Time and Sense,
And of Eternity; and oh! how light
Looked in that truthful hour the earthly scale!
And oh! what strength, when from the penal doom
Nature recoiled, in *His* remembered words—
"I am the Resurrection and the Life!"

 And other words of that Divinest Speaker—
Words to all mourners of all time addressed—
Seemed spoken to me as I went along
In prayerful thought, slow musing on my way—
"*Believe in me. Let not your hearts be troubled.*"
And sure I could have promised in that hour,
But that I knew myself how fallible,
That never more should cross or care of life
Disquiet or distress me. So I came,
Chastened in spirit, to my home again,
Composed and comforted, and crossed the threshold
That day "a wiser, *not* a sadder," woman.

DEPARTURE.

WHEN I go away from my own dear home,
    Let it be at the fall of the leaf,
When the soulless things that to me have been
Like spirits peopling the silent scene,
    Are fading, as if in grief;

When the strains of the summer birds have ceased,
    Or in far-off regions swell—
Oh! let me not hear the blithesome song
Of that blackbird I fed all winter long,
    When I'm taking my last farewell.

The robin-redbreast will come, I know,
    That morn to the window-pane,
To look, as wont, for the scattered feast,
With his large dark eyes:—and that day, at least,
    He shall not look in vain.

Let the autumn wind, when I go away,
    Make moan with its long-drawn breath:
"Fare thee well, sad one!" 'twill seem to say;
"Yet a little while, and a little way,
    And thy feet shall rest in death."

And here and there an evergreen leaf
    I'll gather from shrub and tree,
To take with me wherever I go;
And when this poor head in dust lies low,
    To be laid in the coffin with me.

I go not like one in the strength of youth,
    Who hopes, though the passing cloud
May pour down its icy hail amain,
That summer and sunshine may break out again
    The brighter from sorrow's shroud.

An April morn and a clouded day
    My portion of life hath been :
And darker and darker the evening sky
Stretches before me gloomily,
    To the verge of the closing scene.

Gloomily darkens the evening sky:
    I shall go with a heavy heart.
Yet, would I change, if the power were mine,
One tittle decreed by the will Divine?
    On, no! not a thousandth part.

In my blindness I've wished—in my feebleness wept,
    With a weak, weak woman's wail;
But humbling my heart and its hopes in the dust—
All its hopes that are earthly—I've anchored my trust
    On the strength that can never fail.

—o—

THE CHILD'S UNBELIEF.

"COME hither, my little child, to me!
    Come hither and hearken now.
My poor, poor child! is this a day
For thee to dance, and sport, and play,
    Like blossom on the bough?

"Fair blossom! where's the fostering bough?
    And where's the parent tree?
Stem, root, and branch—all, all laid low—
Almost at once—at one fell blow:
    Dear child! cling close to me,

"My sister's child! for thou shalt grow
    Into my very heart.
But hush that ringing laugh—to me
The silver sound is agony:
    Come, hearken here apart.

"And fold thy little hands in mine,
    Thus standing at my knee;
And look up in my face, and say,
Dost thou remember what to-day
    Weeping I told to thee?

"Alas! my tears are raining fast
    Upon thine orphan head;
And thy sweet eyes are glistening now——
Harry! at last believest thou
    That thy poor mother's dead?"

"No, no! my mother *is not* dead—
    She *can't* be dead, you know.
Oh, aunt! I saw my father die,
All white and cold I saw him lie—
    My mother don't *look so*.

"She cried when I was sent away,
    And I cried very much;
And she was pale, and hung her head,
But all the while her lips were red,
    And soft and warm to touch—

The Child's Unbelief.

"Not like my father's, hard and cold;
    And then *she said*, beside,
She'd come to England soon, you know."
"But, Harry, that was months ago—
    She sickened since and died.

"And the sad news is come to-day—
    Told in *this* letter. See,
'Tis edged and sealed with black." "Oh, dear!
Give me that pretty seal. Look here!
    I'll keep it carefully,

"With all these others, in my box—
    They're all for her. Don't cry;
I'll learn my lessons every day,
That I may have them all to say
    When she comes by-and-by."

"Boy, boy! thy talk will break my heart.
    O Nature! can it be
That thou in his art silent so?
Yet what, poor infant! shouldst thou know
    Of life's great mystery?

"Of time and space—of chance and change—
    Of sin, decay, and death—
What canst thou know, thou sinless one!
Thou yet unstained, unbreathed upon
    By this world's tainting breath?

"A sunbeam all thy little life,
    Thy very being bliss—
Glad creature! who would waken thee
To sense of sin and misery
    From such a dream as this?"

THE GREENWOOD SHRIFT.

OUTSTRETCHED beneath the leafy shade
   Of Windsor forest's deepest glade
     A dying woman lay;
Three little children round her stood,
And there went up from the greenwood
     A woeful wail that day.

"Oh, mother!" was the mingled cry,
"Oh, mother! mother! do not die,
     And leave us all alone."
"My blessed babes!" she strove to say,
But the faint accents died away
     In a low sobbing moan.

And then life struggled hard with death,
And fast and strong she drew her breath,
     And up she raised her head;
And peering through the deep wood maze,
With a long, sharp, unearthly gaze,
     "Will he not come?" she said.

Just then, the parting boughs between,
A little maid's light form was seen,
     All breathless with her speed;
And following close a man came on—
A portly man to look upon—
     Who led a panting steed.

The Greenwood Shrift.

"Mother!" the little maiden cried,
Or e'er she reached the woman's side,
   Or kissed her clay-cold cheek,
"I have not idled in the town,
But long went wandering up and down
   The Minister to seek.

"They told me here, they told me there,
I think they mocked me everywhere;
   And when I found his home,
And begged him, on my bended knee,
To bring his book and come with me,
   Mother! he would not come.

"I told him how you dying lay,
And could not go in peace away
   Without the Minister:
I begged him for dear Christ His sake;
But oh!—my heart was fit to break—
   Mother! he would not stir.

"So, though my tears were blinding me,
I ran back fast as fast could be,
   To come again to you:
When here, close by, this Squire I met,
Who asked so mild what made me fret;
   And when I told him true,

"'I will go with you, child,' he said,
'God sends me to this dying bed.'
   Mother! he's here—hard by."
While thus the little maiden spoke,
The man, his back against an oak,
   Looked on with glistening eye.

The Greenwood Shrift.

The bridle on his neck flung free,
With quivering flank and trembling knee,
    Pressed close his bonny bay;
A statelier man, a statelier steed,
Paced never greensward glade, I rede,
    Than those stood there the day.

So, while the little maiden spoke,
The man, his back against an oak,
    Looked on with glistening eye
And folded arms, and in his look
Something that, like a sermon-book,
    Said—"All is vanity!"

But when the dying woman's face
Turned toward him with a wistful gaze,
    He stept to where she lay,
And kneeling down, bent over her,
Saying—"I am a Minister;
    My sister, let us pray."

And well, withouten book or stole
(God's words were printed on his soul),
    Into the dying ear
He poured as 'twere an angel's strain
The things that unto life pertain,
    And death's dark shadows clear.

He spoke of sinners' lost estate,
In Christ renewed, regenerate;
    Of God's most blest decree,
That not a single soul shall die
Who turns repentant, with the cry,
    "Be merciful to me!"

The Greenwood Shrift.

Then, as the spirit ebbed away,
He raised his hands and eyes to pray
    That peaceful it might pass;
And then——the orphans' wail alone
Was heard, as they knelt, every one,
    Close round on the green grass.

Such was the sight their wondering eyes
Beheld, in heart-struck mute surprise,
    Who reined their coursers back,
Just as they found the long astray,
Who, in the heat of chase that day,
    Had wandered from the track.

Back each man reined his pawing steed,
And lighted down, as if agreed,
    In silence at his side;
And there, uncovered all, they stood:
It was a wholesome sight and good,
    That day, for mortal pride.

For of the noblest of the land
Was that deep-hushed, bare-headed band;
    And, central in the ring,
By that dead pauper on the ground,
Her ragged orphans clinging round,
    Knelt their anointed King!

THE WARNING.

THERE'S bloom upon the lady's cheek,
    There's brightness in her eye:
Who says the sentence is gone forth
    That that fair thing must die?—

Must die before the flowering lime,
    Out yonder, sheds its leaf:
Can this thing be, O human flower!
    Thy blossoming so brief?

Nay, nay: 'tis but a passing cloud;
    Thou dost but droop awhile:
There's life (long years), and love, and joy
    (Whole ages), in that smile—

In the gay call that to thy knee
    Brings quick that loving child,
Who looks up in those laughing eyes,
    With his large eyes so mild.

Yet thou art doomed—art dying. All
    The coming hour foresee,
But, in love's cowardice, withhold
    The warning word from thee.

God help thee, and be merciful!
    His strength is with the weak;
Through babes and sucklings the Most High
    Hath oft vouchsafed to speak,

The Warning.

And speaketh now :—"O Mother, dear!"
    Whispers the little child—
And there is trouble in his eyes,
    Those large blue eyes so mild—

"O Mother, dear! they say that soon,
    When here I seek for thee,
I shall not find thee; nor out there
    Under the old oak tree;

"Nor upstairs in the nursery;
    Nor anywhere, they say.
Where wilt thou go to, Mother, dear?
    Oh, do not go away!"

There was deep silence—a long hush—
    And then the child's low sob;
Her quivering eyelids close; one hand
    Holds down the heart's quick throb,

And the lips move, though sound is none:
    That inward voice is prayer;
And hark!—"Thy will, O Lord! be done."
    And tears are trickling there,

Down that fair cheek, on that young head,
    And round her neck he clings;
And child and mother murmur out
    Unutterable things:

He half unconscious—she heart-struck
    With sudden, solemn truth,
That numbered are her days on earth,
    Her shroud prepared in youth;

That all in life her heart holds dear
   God calls her to resign.
She hears—feels—trembles—but looks up,
   And sighs—" Thy will be mine ! ".

---o---

THE THREE FRIENDS.

STANZAS ACCOMPANYING A PICTURE.

WE three were loving friends!—a lowly life
   Of humble peace, obscure content, we led:
Stealing away, withouten noise or strife,
   Like some small streamlet in its mossy bed.

We had our joys in common—wisdom, wit,
   And learned lore, had little share in those:
Thus, by the winter fire we used to sit,
   Or in the summer evening's warm repose.

At our sweet bowery window, opening down
   To the green grass, beneath the flowering lime,
When the deep curfew from the distant town
   Came mellowed, like the voice of olden time ;

And our grave neighbour, from the barn hard by,
   The great grey owl, sailed out on soundless wings,
And the pale stars, like beams of memory,
   Brightened as twilight veiled all earthly things.

'Twas then we used to sit, as pictured *thus*—
   My pillow, as in childhood, still the same,

Those venerable knees, and close to us,
  Old Ranger, pressing oft his jealous claim.

And then I loved to feel that gentle hand
  Laid like a blessing on my head—to hear
The "auld-warld" stories, ever at command,
  By all but *her* forgotten many a year;

And then we talked together of the days
  We both remembered—and of those who slept—
And the old dog looked up with wistful gaze,
  As if he, too, that faithful record kept.

We three were loving friends!—now one is gone,
  And one—poor feeble thing!—declineth fast;
And well I wot, the days are drawing on
  Will find me here, the lonely and the last;

But not to tarry long; and when I go,
  The stranger's hand will have dominion here,
And lay thy walls, my peaceful dwelling! low,
  As my last lodging in the churchyard near,

    1824.

———o———

MY GARDEN.

I LOVE my Garden!—dearly love
  That little spot of ground!
There's not, methinks—though I may err
In partial pride—a pleasanter,
  In all the country round!

My Garden.

The smooth green turf winds gently there,
    With no ungraceful bend,
Round many a bed and many a border,
Where, gaily grouped in sweet disorder,
    Young Flora's darlings blend.

Spring! Summer! Autumn!—of all three,
    Whose reign is loveliest there?
Oh! is not she who paints the ground,
When its frost fetters are unbound,
    The fairest of the fair?

I gaze upon her violet beds,
    Laburnums, golden-tressed;
Her flower-spiked almond—breathe perfume
From lilac and syringa bloom,
    And cry, "I love Spring best!"

But Summer comes, with all her pomp
    Of fragrance, beauty, bliss!—
And from amidst her bower of roses,
I sigh, as purple evening closes,
    "What season equals this?"

That pageant passeth by. Comes next
    Brown Autumn in her turn;—
Oh! not unwelcome cometh she;
The parchèd earth luxuriously
    Drinks from her dewy urn.

And she hath flowers, and fragrance too,
    Peculiarly her own;
Asters of every hue—perfume,
Spiced rich with clematis and broom,
    And mignonette late blown.

Then if some lingering rose I spy
　　Reclining languidly,
Or the bright laurel's glossy green,—
Dear Autumn! my whole heart, I ween,
　　Leaps up for love of thee!

Oh, yes!—I love my garden well,
　　And find employment there;—
Employment sweet; for many an hour,
In tending every shrub and flower
　　With still unwearied care.

I prop the weakly—prune the rude—
　　Scatter the various seeds—
Clear out intruders,—yet of *those*
Oft sparing, what the florist knows
　　To be but gaudy weeds.

But when my task—my pleasant task!—
　　Is ended for the day—
Sprinkled o'er every sun-bowed flower
The artificial evening shower,
　　Then oftentimes I stray—

(Inherent is the love of change
　　In human hearts)—far, far
Beyond the garden-gate;—the bound
That clips my little Eden round,
　　Chance for my leading star;

Through hollow lanes or coppice paths,
　　By hill or hawthorn fence,
O'er thymy commons, clover fields,
Where every step I take reveals
　　Some charm of sight or sense.

My Garden.

The winding path brings suddenly
    A rustic bridge in sight;
Beneath it, gushing brightly out,
The rivulet, where speckled trout
    Leap in the circling light.

Pale water-lilies float thereon,
    The Naiads' loveliest wreath!
The adders' tongues dip down to drink;
The flag peers high above the brink,
    From her long slender sheath.

There, on the greensward, an old oak
    Stands singly. One, I trow,
Whose mighty shadow spread as wide,
When they were in their prime, who died
    A hundred years ago.

A single ewe, with her twin lambs,
    Stands the grey trunk beside;
Others lie clustering in the shade,
Or, down the windings of the glade,
    Are scattered far and wide.

Two mossy thorns, o'er yonder stile,
    A bowery archway rise;—
Oh, what a flood of fragrance thence
Breathes out!—Behind that hazel fence
    A flowering bean-field lies.

The shadowy path winds gently on,
    That hazel fence beneath;
The wild-rose, and the woodbine there
Shoot up, festooning high in air
    Their oft-entangled wreath.

My Garden.

The path winds on—on either side
    Walled in by hedges high ;
Their boughs so thickly arching over,
That scarce one speck you can discover—
    One speck of the blue sky!

A lovely gloom! It pleaseth me
    And lonely Philomel.
Hark! the enchantress sings!—that strain
Dies with a tremulous fall!—again—
    Oh, what a gushing swell!

Darker and darker still the road,
    Scarce lit by twilight glances ;—
Darker and darker still——But, see!
Yonder, on that young aspen-tree,
    A darting sunbeam dances.

Another gems the bank below
    With emeralds! Into one
They blend—unite——one emerald sea!
And last, in all his majesty,
    Breaks through the setting sun!

And I am breathless, motionless,
    Mute with delight and love!
My very being seems to blend
With all around me—to ascend
    To the great Source above.

I feel I am a spark struck out
    From an eternal flame ;
A part of the stupendous whole,
His work, who breathed a deathless soul
    Into this mortal frame.

And *they* shall perish—all these things—
   Darkness shall quench this ball:
Death-throes this solid earth shall rive,
Yet I—frail thing of dust!—survive
   The final wreck of all.

"Wake up my glory! lute and harp!"
   Be vocal every chord;
Lo! all His works in concert sing,
"Praise, praise to the Eternal King,"
   The Universal Lord!

Oh, powerless will! oh, languid voice!
   Weak words! imperfect lays!
Yet, could His works alone inspire
The feelings that attune my lyre
   To these faint notes of praise!

Not to the charms of tasteful art
   That I am cold or dull;
I gaze on all the graceful scene—
The clustering flowers, the velvet green—
   And cry, "How beautiful!"

But when to Nature's book I turn,
   The page *she* spreads abroad;
Tears only to mine eyes that steal,
Bear witness that I see and feel
   The mighty hand of God!

THE YOUNG GREY HEAD.

GRIEF hath been known to turn the young head
   grey—
To silver over in a single day
The bright locks of the beautiful, their prime
Scarcely o'erpast: as in the fearful time
Of Gallia's madness, that discrownèd head
Serene, that on the accursèd altar bled,
Miscalled of Liberty. Oh, martyred Queen!
What must the sufferings of that night have been?—
That one—that sprinkled thy fair tresses o'er
With Time's untimely snow! But now no more,
Lovely, august, unhappy one, of thee—
I have to tell an humbler history;
A village tale, whose only charm, in sooth,
If any, will be sad and simple truth.

"Mother," quoth Ambrose to his thrifty dame—
So oft our peasant's use his wife to name,
"Father" and "Master" to himself applied,
As life's grave duties matronise the bride—
"Mother," quoth Ambrose, as he faced the north,
With hard-set teeth, before he issued forth
To his day labour, from the cottage door—
"I'm thinking that to-night, if not before,
There'll be wild work. Dost hear old Chewton* roar?
It's brewing up down westward; and look there!
One of those sea-gulls—ay, there goes a pair.

* A fresh-water spring rushing into the sea called Chewton Bunny.

And such a sudden thaw! If rain comes on,
As threats, the waters will be out anon.
That path by the ford's a nasty bit of way—
Best let the young ones bide from school to-day."

"Do, mother, do!" the quick-eared urchins cried,
Two little lasses, to the father's side
Close clinging, as they looked from him, to spy
The answering language of the mother's eye.
There was denial, and she shook her head:
"Nay, nay—no harm will come to them," she said,
"The mistress lets them off, these short dark days,
An hour the earlier; and our Liz, she says,
May quite be trusted—and I know 'tis true—
To take care of herself and Jenny too.
And so she ought—*she* seven come first of May,
Two years the oldest: and they give away
The Christmas bounty at the school to-day."

The mother's will was law—alas for her
That hapless day, poor soul! *She* could not err,
Thought Ambrose; and his little fair-haired Jane,
Her namesake, to his heart he hugged again,
When each had had her turn, she clinging so
As if that day she could not let him go.
But Labour's sons must snatch a hasty bliss
In nature's tenderest mood. One last fond kiss—
"God bless my little maids!" the father said,
And cheerly went his way to win their bread.
Then might be seen, the playmate parent gone,
What looks demure the sister pair put on—
Not of the mother as afraid or shy,
Or questioning the love that could deny,
But simply, as their simple training taught,

In quiet, plain straightforwardness of thought
(Submissively resigned the hope of play),
Towards the serious business of the day.

   To me there's something touching, I confess,
In the grave look of early thoughtfulness,
Seen often in some little childish face
Among the poor. Not that wherein we trace
(Shame to our land, our rulers, and our race!)
The unnatural sufferings of the factory child,
But a staid quietness, reflective, mild,
Betokening, in the depths of those young eyes,
Sense of life's cares, without its miseries.

   So to the mother's charge, with thoughtful brow,
The docile Lizzy stood attentive now,
Proud of her years and of imputed sense,
And prudence justifying confidence;
And little Jenny, more demurely still,
Beside her waited the maternal will.
So standing hand in hand, a lovelier twain
Gainsborough ne'er painted; no, nor he of Spain,
Glorious Murillo!—and by contrast shown
More beautiful. The younger little one,
With large blue eyes, and silken ringlets fair,
By nut-brown Lizzy, with smooth parted hair,
Sable and glossy as the raven's wing,
And lustrous eyes as dark.
                    "Now, mind and bring
Jenny safe home," the mother said—"don't stay
To pull a bough or berry by the way:
And when you come to cross the ford, hold fast
Your little sister's hand till you're quite past—
That plank's so crazy, and so slippery,

If not o'erflowed, the stepping-stones will be.
But you're good children, steady as old folk—
I'd trust ye anywhere." Then Lizzy's cloak,
A good grey duffle, lovingly she tied,
And amply little Jenny's lack supplied
With her own warmest shawl. "Be sure," said she,
"To wrap it round and knot it carefully,
Like this, when you come home, just leaving free
One hand to hold by. Now, make haste away—
Good will to school, and then good right to play."

Was there no sinking at the mother's heart,
When, all equipt, they turned them to depart?
When down the lane she watched them as they
    went,
Till out of sight, was no forefeeling sent
Of coming ill? In truth I cannot tell:
Such warnings *have been sent*, we know full well,
And must believe—believing that they are—
In mercy then—to rouse—restrain—prepare.

And, now I mind me, something of the kind
Did surely haunt that day the mother's mind,
Making it irksome to bide all alone
By her own quiet hearth. Though never known
For idle gossipry was Jenny Gray,
Yet so it was, that morn she could not stay
At home with her own thoughts, but took her way
To her next neighbour's half a loaf to borrow—
Yet might her store have lasted out the morrow.
And with the loan obtained, she lingered still:
Said she—" My master, if he'd had his will,
Would have kept back our little ones from school
This dreadful morning; and I'm such a fool,

Since they've been gone, I've wished them back. But then
It won't do in such things to humour men,
Our Ambrose specially. If let alone
He'd spoil those wenches. But it's coming on,
That storm he said was brewing, sure enough.
Well, what of that? To think what idle stuff
Will come into one's head! and here with you
I stop, as if I'd nothing else to do—
And they'll come home drowned rats. I must be gone
To get dry things, and set the kettle on."

His day's work done, three mortal miles and more
Lay between Ambrose and his cottage door.
A weary way, God wot! for weary wight.
But yet far off the curling smoke's in sight
From his own chimney, and his heart feels light.
How pleasantly the humble homestead stood,
Down the green lane by sheltering Shirley Wood!
How sweet the wafting of the evening breeze
In spring-time, from his two old cherry-trees,
Sheeted with blossom! And in hot July,
From the brown moor-track, shadowless and dry,
How grateful the cool covert to regain
Of his own *avenue*, that shady lane,
With the white cottage, in a slanting glow
Of sunset glory, gleaming bright below,
And jasmine porch, his rustic portico!

With what a thankful gladness in his face
(Silent heart-homage—plant of special grace!),
At the lane's entrance, slackening oft his pace,
Would Ambrose send a loving look before;
Conceiting the caged blackbird at the door,

The very blackbird strained its little throat
In welcome with a more rejoicing note;
And honest Tinker, dog of doubtful breed,
All bristle, back, and tail, but "good at need,"
Pleasant his greeting to the accustomed ear;
But of all welcomes, pleasantest, most dear,
The ringing voices, like sweet silver bells,
Of his two little ones. How fondly swells
The father's heart, as, dancing up the lane,
Each clasps a hand in her small hand again,
And each must tell her tale, and "say her say,"
Impeding, as she leads, with sweet delay
(Childhood's blest thoughtlessness) his onward way.

And when the winter day closed in so fast,
Scarce for his task would dreary daylight last;
And in all weathers, driving sleet and snow,
Home by that bare, bleak moor-track must he go,
Darkling and lonely. Oh! the blessed sight—
His pole-star—of that little twinkling light
From one small window, through the leafless trees,
Glimmering so fitfully, no eye but his
Had spied it so far off. And sure was he,
Entering the lane, a steadier beam to see,
Ruddy and broad as peat-fed hearth could pour,
Streaming to meet him from the open door.
Then, though the blackbird's welcome was unheard,
Silenced by winter, note of summer bird
Still hailed him—from no mortal fowl alive,
But from the cuckoo-clock just striking five.
And Tinker's ear and Tinker's nose were keen—
Off started he, and then a form was seen
Darkening the doorway; and a smaller sprite,
And then another, peered into the night,

Ready to follow free on Tinker's track,
But for the mother's hand that held her back.
And yet a moment—a few steps—and there,
Pulled o'er the threshold by that eager pair,
He sits by his own hearth, in his own chair;
Tinker takes post beside, with eyes that say,
"Master, we've done our business for the day."
The kettle sings, the cat in chorus purrs,
The busy housewife with her tea-things stirs;
The door's made fast, the old stuff curtain drawn.
How the hail clatters! Let it clatter on.
How the wind raves and rattles! What cares he?
Safe housed, and warm beneath his own roof-tree,
With a wee lassie prattling on each knee.

Such was the hour—hour sacred and apart—
Warmed in expectancy the poor man's heart.
Summer and winter, as his toil he plied,
To him and his the literal doom applied,
Pronouuced on Adam. But the bread was sweet,
So earned for such dear mouths. The weary feet,
Hope-shod, stept lightly on the homeward way.
So specially it fared with Ambrose Gray
That time I tell of. He had worked all day
At a great clearing, vigorous stroke on stroke
Striking, till, when he stopt, his back seemed broke,
And the strong arm dropt nerveless. What of that?
There was a treasure hidden in his hat,
A plaything for the young ones. He had found
A dormouse nest, the living ball coiled round
For its long winter sleep; and all his thought,
As he trudged stoutly homeward, was of nought
But the glad wonderment in Jenny's eyes,
And graver Lizzy's quieter surprise,

When he should yield, by guess, and kiss, and prayer,
Hard won, the frozen captive to their care.

'Twas a wild evening—wild and rough. "I knew,"
Thought Ambrose; "those unlucky gulls spoke true,
And Gaffer Chewton never growls for nought.
I should be mortal 'mazed now if I thought
My little maids were not safe housed before
That blinding hail-storm—ay, this hour and more.
Unless by that old crazy bit of board,
They've not passed dry-foot over Shallow-ford,
That I'll be bound for, swollen as it must be . . .
Well! if my mistress had been ruled by me . . ."
But checking the half-thought as heresy,
He looked out for the home-star. There it shone,
And with a gladdened heart he hastened on.

He's in the lane again—and there below
Streams from the open doorway that red glow,
Which warms him but to look at. For his prize
Cautious he feels—all safe and snug it lies.
"Down, Tinker! down, old boy!—not quite so free:
The thing thou sniffest is no game for thee.
But what's the meaning?—no look-out to-night!
No living soul astir! Pray God all's right!
Who's flittering round the peat-stack in such weather?
Mother!" You might have felled him with a feather
When the short answer to his loud "Hillo!"
And hurried question—"Are they come?"—was—
    "No!"

To throw his tools down—hastily unhook
The old cracked lantern from its dusty nook,
And, while he lit it, speak a cheering word

The Young Grey Head.

That almost choked him, and was scarcely heard,
Was but a moment's act, and he was gone
To where a fearful foresight led him on.
Passing a neighbour's cottage in his way—
Mark Fenton's—him he took with short delay
To bear him company—for who could say
What need might be? They struck into the track
The children should have taken coming back
From school that day; and many a call and shout
Into the pitchy darkness they sent out,
And, by the lantern-light, peered all about,
In every roadside thicket, hole, and nook,
Till suddenly—as nearing now the brook—
Something brushed past them. That was Tinker's bark.
Unheeded he had followed in the dark
Close at his master's heels, but, swift as light,
Darted before them now. "Be sure he's right—
He's on the track," cried Ambrose. "Hold the light
Low down—he's making for the water. Hark!
I know that whine—the old dog's found them, Mark."
So speaking, breathlessly he hurried on
Toward the old crazy foot-bridge. It was gone!
And all his dull contracted light could show
Was the black void and dark swollen stream below.
"Yet there's life somewhere—more than Tinker's whine—
That's sure," said Mark. "So, let the lantern shine
Down yonder. There's the dog—and hark!"—
                                        "Oh, dear!"
And a low sob came faintly on the ear,
Mocked by the sobbing gust. Down, quick as thought,
Into the stream leapt Ambrose, where he caught
Fast hold of something—a dark huddled heap,

Half in the water, where 'twas scarce knee-deep
For a tall man, and half above it, propped
By some old ragged side-piles that had stopt
Endways the broken plank when it gave way
With the two little ones that luckless day.
"My babes! my lambkins!" was the father's cry.
One little voice made answer—" Here am I!"
'Twas Lizzy's. There she crouched, with face as white,
More ghastly by the flickering lantern-light,
Than sheeted corpse. The pale blue lips, drawn tight,
Wide parted, showing all the pearly teeth,
And eyes on some dark object underneath,
Washed by the turbid water, fixed like stone—
One arm and hand stretched out, and rigid grown,
Grasping, as in the death-gripe, Jenny's frock.
There she lay drowned. Could *he* sustain that shock,
The doating father? Where's the unriven rock
Can bide such blasting in its flintiest part
As that soft, sentient thing—the human heart?

    They lifted her from out her watery bed.
Its covering gone, the lovely little head
Hung like a broken snowdrop all aside,
And one small hand. The mother's shawl was tied,
Leaving *that* free, about the child's small form,
As was her last injunction—"*fast* and warm"—
Too well obeyed—too fast! A fatal hold
Affording to the scrag by a thick fold,
That caught and pinned her in the river's bed,
While through the reckless water overhead
Her life-breath bubbled up.
                      "She might have lived,
Struggling like Lizzy," was the thought that rived
The wretched mother's heart when she knew all,

"But for my foolishness about that shawl.
And Master would have kept them back the day;
But I was wilful—driving them away
In such wild weather!"
      Thus the tortured heart
Unnaturally against itself takes part,
Driving the sharp edge deeper of a woe
Too deep already. They had raised her now,
And parting the wet ringlets from her brow,
To that, and the cold cheek, and lips as cold,
The father glued his warm ones, ere they rolled
Once more the fatal shawl, her winding-sheet,
About the precious clay. One heart still beat
Warmed by *his heart's* blood. To his *only child*
He turned him, but her piteous moaning mild
Pierced him afresh—and now she knew him not.
"Mother!" she murmured, "who says I forgot?
Mother! indeed, indeed, I kept fast hold,
And tied the shawl quite close—she can't be cold—
But she won't move—we slipt—I don't know how—
But I held on—and I'm so weary now—
And it's so dark and cold—oh, dear! oh, dear!—
And she won't move—if daddy was but here!"

  * * * * * *

Poor lamb! she wandered in her mind, 'twas clear;
But soon the piteous murmur died away,
And quiet in her father's arms she lay:
They their dead burthen had resigned to take
The living so near lost. For her dear sake,
And one at home, he armed himself to bear
His misery like a man. With tender care,
Doffing his coat her shivering form to fold—

His neighbour bearing *that* which felt no cold—
He clasped her close; and so, with little said,
Homeward they bore the living and the dead.
From Ambrose Gray's poor cottage, all that night,
Shone fitfully a little shifting light,
Above—below: for all were watchers there,
Save one sound sleeper. *Her*, parental care,
Parental watchfulness, availed not now.
But in the young survivor's throbbing brow
And wandering eyes delirious fever burned,
And all night long from side to side she turned,
Piteously 'plaining like a wounded dove,
With now and then the murmur—"She won't move!'
And lo! when morning, as in mockery, bright
Shone on that pillow—passing strange the sight—
That young head's raven hair was streaked with white!
No idle fiction this. Such things have been,
We know. And now I tell what I have seen.

Life struggled long with death in that small frame
But it was strong, and conquered. All became
As it had been with the poor family—
All—saving that which never more might be:
There was an empty place—they were but three.

LITTLE LEONARD'S "GOOD-NIGHT."

"GOOD-NIGHT! good-night! I go to sleep,"
    Murmured the little child;—
And oh! the ray of heaven that broke
On the sweet lips that faintly spoke
    That soft "Good-night," and smiled!

That angel smile! that loving look
    From the dim closing eyes!
The peace of that pure brow! But there—
Ay, on that brow, so young! so fair!—
    An awful shadow lies.

The gloom of evening—of the boughs
    That o'er yon window wave?—
Nay, nay; within these silent walls,
A deeper, darker shadow falls,
    The twilight of the Grave—

The twilight of the Grave—for still
    Fast comes the fluttering breath—
One fading smile—one look of love—
A murmur—as from brooding dove—
    "Good-night."——And this is Death!

Oh! who hath called thee "Terrible!"
    Mild Angel! most benign!
Could mother's fondest lullaby
Have laid to rest more blissfully
    That sleeping babe than thine!

Yet this *is* Death—the doom for all
    Of Adam's race decreed—

"But this poor lamb! this little one!—
What had the guiltless creature done?"
   Unhappy heart! take heed;

Though He is merciful as just
   Who hears that fond appeal—
He will not break the bruisèd reed,
He will not search the wounds that bleed—
   He only wounds to heal.

"Let little children come to me,"
   He cried, and to His breast
Folded them tenderly—To-day
He calls thine unshorn lamb away
   To that securest rest!

———o———

"HOW SWIFT IS A GLANCE OF THE MIND!"

AN EXILE'S SONG.

*"When I think of my own native land,
In a moment I seem to be there."*

THAT flower, that flower! Oh, pluck that flower for me!
   There, in the running stream,
   Its silvery* clusters gleam:
     Oh! give it me!
The same! the very same! I knew it well,
   Last seen so long ago. Oh, simple flower,
   That sight of thee should waken up this hour
     Thoughts more than tongue can tell!

       * The Buckbean.

A moment since, and I was calm and cold—
    Cold as this world to me,
    With all its pageantry,
        Grown stale and old.
Now the warm blood, through every throbbing vein
    Fast hurrying, mantles over cheek and brow,
    Like youth and hope rekindling—ebbing now
        To the full heart again:

Leaving a paler cheek—a glistening eye
    With watery gaze fixed fast
    On visions of the past;
        Oh! where am I?
At home, at home again in mine own land:
    Its mountain streams are murmuring in mine ear,
    And thrilling voices from loud lips I hear.
        There—there the loving band.

Mine own long lost!—Oh! take the weary one
    To weep on some dear breast
    This agony to rest—
        On thine, my son!
Thou answerest not—none answer me—that cry
    Was from mine own sad heart; and they are gone—
    And at my feet the little brook flows on
        Tranquilly—tranquilly.

No mountain streamlet of my native land;
    Yet doth its voice to me
    Sound sweet and soothingly;
        And in mine hand,
Of those pale flowers, now gemmed with tears, I hold
    Henceforth to memory sacred:—from this hour
    That they've awakened with such wondrous power,
        Dreams of the days of old.

ON THE REMOVAL OF SOME FAMILY PORTRAITS.

SILENT friends! fare ye well—
   Shadows! adieu.
Living friends long I've lost,
   Now I lose you.

Bitter tears many I've shed,
   Ye've seen them flow;
Dreary hours many I've sped,
   Full well ye know.

Yet in my loneliness,
   Kindly, methought,
Still ye looked down on me,
   Mocking me not

With light speech and hollow words,
   Grating so sore
The sad heart, with many ills
   Sick to the core.

Then, if my clouded skies
   Brightened awhile,
Seemed your soft serious eyes
   Almost to smile.

Silent friends! fare ye well—
   Shadows! adieu.
Living friends long I've lost,
   Now I lose you.

On the Removal of some Family Portraits.

Taken from hearth and board,
        When all were gone;
I looked up at you, and felt
        Not quite alone.

Not quite companionless,
        While in each face
Met me familiar
        The stamp of my race.

Thine, gentle ancestress!
        Dove-eyed and fair,
Melting in sympathy
        Oft for my care.

Grim Knight and stern visaged!
        Yet could I see,
Smoothing that furrowed face,
        Good-will to me.

Bland looks were beaming
        Upon me, I knew,
Fair sir!—bonnie lady!—
        From you, and from you.

Little think happy ones,
        Heart-circled round,
How fast to senseless things
        Hearts may be bound;

How when the living prop's
        Mouldered and gone,
Heart-strings, low trailing left,
        Clasp the cold stone.

On the Removal of some Family Portraits.

Silent friends! fare ye well—
        Shadows! adieu.
Living friends long I've lost,
        Now I lose you.

Often, when spirit-vexed,
        Weary and worn,
To your quiet faces, mute
        Friends, would I turn.

Soft as I gazed on them,
        Soothing as balm,
Lulling the passion-storm,
        Stole your deep calm—

Till, as I longer looked,
        Surely, methought,
Ye read and replied to
        My questioning thought.

"Daughter," ye softly said—
        " Peace to thine heart:
We too—yes, daughter! have
        Been as thou art,

"Tossed on the troubled waves,
        Life's stormy sea;
Chance and change manifold
        Proving like thee.

" Hope-lifted—doubt-depressed—
        Seeing in part—
Tried—troubled—tempted—
        Sustained as thou art—

"*Our* God is *thy* God—what He
    Willeth is best—
Trust him as we trusted: then
    Rest, as we rest."

Silent friends! fare ye well—
    Shadows! adieu—
One Friend abideth still
    All changes through.

—*o*—

SONNET.—1818.

DARK rolling clouds, in wild confusion driven,
    Obscure the full-orbed moon. In all the heaven
One only star—the appointed evening light—
Beams mildly forth; like friendly Pharos bright,
That, kindled on some towering summit, streams
Wide o'er the ocean-paths. Its far-off beams
First seen by him who on the silent deck
Paces his lonely watch—a glimmering speck,
Doubtful in distance. But his homeward eye
Is keen the faithful beacon to descry,
And mine, like his, impatient to explore—
With friends and kindred thronged—the distant shore,
Is fixed on that lone star, whose lovely ray
Points to a happier home the heavenward way.

WILD FLOWERS.

YE who courtly beauty prize,
　　Cast not here your scornful eyes
Nature's lowly children we,
Bred on bank, in brake, on lea,
By the meadow runlet's brink,
In the tall cliff's craggy chink,
On the seashore's arid shingle,
On bleak moor, in bosky dingle,
On old tower and ruined wall,
By the sparkling waterfall.

Not a hue of gaudier glow,
Not a streak to art we owe;
Never hand but Nature's own—
Nature's "sweet and cunning one"—
Hath imparted charm and grace
To our unaspiring race:
All her elements of might,
Common air and common light,
Shower and sunshine, mist and dew;
And her labourers—blithe ones too—
All unhired, for love she finds—
Bees, and birds, and wandering winds.

Courtly scorners! not for ye
Bloom our tribes of low degree.
Stately aloe, tuberose tall,
Fitly grace baronial hall,
Flaunting in exotic pride,
Sculptured nymph or fawn beside,

Wild Flowers.

From marble vase on terrace wide,
Where jewelled robes sweep rustling by,
And lordly idlers lounge and sigh ;—
There intrude not such as we,
Commoners of low degree.
Yet have we our lovers too,
Hearts to holy Nature true,
Such as find in all her ways
Objects for delight and praise,
From the cedar, straight and tall,
To " the hyssop on the wall."

Favoured mortals! to your eyes,
All unveiled, an Eden lies,
Hidden from the worldling's view ;
Wells of water gush for you
Where his sealèd sight doth spy
Nought but dull aridity.
Hither come—to you we'll tell
Where our sweetest sisters dwell—
Show you every secret cell
Where the coy take sanctuary,
" Pale maids that unmarried die "—
Primroses, and paler yet,
The unstainèd, odorous violet.
Hither come, and you shall see
Where the loveliest lilies be—
They through forest vistas gleaming
(Azure clouds of heaven's own seeming)—
They their snowy heads that hide,
Cowering by the coppice side—
They that stand in nodding ranks,
All along the river's banks,
Golden daffodils ; and they—

Brightest of the bright array—
With a swan-like grace that glide,
Anchored on the waveless tide,—
These and flowery myriads more,
All their charms—a countless store—
All their sweets shall yield to thee,
Nature's faithful votary!

Though we grace not lordly halls,
Yet, on rustic festivals,
Who than we are fitlier seen
Flaunting o'er the village green?
Many a kerchief deck we there,
Many a maiden's nut-brown hair;
Many a straw hat, plaited neat
By shepherd boy, we make complete
With cowslip cark'net:—Then to see
With what an air, how jauntily
On his curled pate 'tis stuck awry,
To snare some cottage beauty's eye!

Joyous childhood, roving free,
With our sweet bells greedily
Both his chubby hands doth fill.
Welcome plunderer! pluck at will,
Nature's darling! dear to thee
More than garden tribes are we.
Pluck at will enough to deck,
Boy, thy favourite lambkin's neck.

Pineth some pale wretch away
In prison cell, where cheerful day
Only through the deep-set bars
Beams obliquely, and the stars

Scarce can glance a pitying eye
On the poor soul's misery?
Haply on some lodgment nigh,
Mossy bastion's mouldering edge,
Loophole chink, or grating ledge,
One of us (some fragrant thing)
Taketh stand, and thence doth fling
On the kind air soft perfume
Down to that dark prison room.
Entering with the balmy gale,
Thoughts of some dear native vale,
Some sweet home by mountain stream,
On the captive's soul may gleam,
Wafting him, in fondest dream,
To the grass-plat far away,
Where his little children play.

On the poor man's grave we're found,
Honouring the unhonoured ground;
To the grave—the grave, for aye—
Reverential dues we pay,
When all thought hath passed away
From all living, long ago,
Of the dust that sleeps below;
From the sunken hillock gone,
E'en the cold memorial stone,
Unforsaking, we alone
Year by year fresh tribute spread
O'er the long-forgotten dead.

TO LITTLE MARY.

I'M bidden, little Mary!
   To write verses upon thee;
I'd fain obey the bidding
   If it rested but with me:
But the Mistresses I'm bound to—
   Nine Ladies hard to please—
Of all their stores poetic
   So closely keep the keys,
It's only now and then,
   By good luck, as one may say,
That a couplet or a rhyme or two
   Falls fairly in my way.

Fruit forced is never half so sweet
   As that comes quite in season—
But some folks must be satisfied
   With rhyme in spite of reason.
So, Muses! now befriend me,
   Albeit of help so chary,
To string the pearls of poesie
   For loveliest little Mary.

And yet, ye pagan Damsels!
   Not over fond am I
To invoke your haughty favours,
   Your fount of Castaly.
I've sipt a purer fountain,
   I've decked a holier shrine,

To Little Mary.

I own a mightier Mistress—
  O Nature! *Thou* art mine.
And Feeling's fount than Castaly
  Yields waters more divine!

And only to that well-head,
  Sweet Mary! I'll resort,
For just an artless verse or two,
  A simple strain and short,
Befitting well a Pilgrim
  Wayworn with earthly strife,
To offer thee, young Traveller!
  In the morning track of life.

There's many a one will tell thee
  'Tis all with roses gay—
There's many a one will tell thee
  'Tis thorny all the way—
Deceivers are they every one,
  Dear Child! who thus pretend;
God's ways are not unequal—
  Make Him thy trusted friend,
And many a path of pleasantness
  He'll clear away for thee,
However dark and intricate
  The labyrinth may be.

I need not wish thee beauty—
  I need not wish thee grace—
Already both are budding
  In that infant form and face.
I will not wish thee grandeur—
  I will not wish thee wealth—

But only a contented heart,
   Peace—competence—and health—
Fond friends to love thee dearly,
   And honest friends to chide,
And faithful ones to cleave to thee,
   Whatever may betide.

And now, my little Mary!
   If better things remain,
Unheeded in my blindness,
   Unnoticed in my strain,
I'll sum them up succinctly,
   In "English undefiled,"
My mother tongue's best benison,—
   God bless thee—precious Child!

SONNET.—1821.

STAY, flaming chariot! fiery coursers, stay,
   Soft gleams of setting sunshine, that doth cast
   A lustrous line along the dark wide waste!
Oh! wherefore must ye fade so swift away?
Wherefore, oh! wherefore, at the close of day
   Shine out so glorious, when Night's sable pall
   Will drop around so soon, and cover all?
Beautiful beam! bright traveller! stay, oh, stay!
And let my spirit on your parting ray
   Glide from this world of error, doubt, distress—
   (Oh! I am weary of its emptiness)—
To happier worlds, where there is peace for aye,
   Peace! less abiding here than Noah's dove,
   When we shall never part from those we love!

THE LEGEND OF THE LIDO.

I.

HE stood before the Signori,
   With a truthful look and bold,
A look of calm simplicity,
   That fisherman poor and old;
Though every face, with a gathering frown
And a searching glance, looked darkly down
   While his wonderful tale he told.

II.

And though a voice from—he knew not where
   (For none beside him stood),
Breathed in his very ear "Beware!"
   In a tone might have froze his blood,
He but crossed himself as he glanced around,
But faltered neither for sight nor sound,
   For he knew that his cause was good.

III.

"I tell the truth—I tell no lie,"
   Old Gian Battista said;
"But hear me out, and patiently,
   Signori wise and dread;
And if I fail sure proof to bring
How I came by this golden ring"
(He held it high, that all might see),
"There are the cells and the Piombi—
   Or—off with this old grey head.

IV.

"Ye know—all know—what fearful work
   The winds and waves have driven
These three days past. That darkness murk
   So shrouded earth and heaven,
We scarce could tell if sun or moon
Looked down on island or lagune,
Or if 'twere midnight or high noon;
And yells and shrieks were in the air,
As if with spirits in despair
   The very fiends had striven.

V.

"And busy, sure enough, were they,
   As soon ye'll understand;
Many believed the doomful day
   Of Venice was at hand:
For high o'er every level known,
The rising flood came crashing on,
Till not a sea-mark old was seen,
Nor of the striplet islets green
   A speck of hard, dry sand.

VI.

"'Well, Gian and his old boat,' quoth I,
   'Together must sink or swim.
They've both seen service out wellnigh,
   Half foundered, plank and limb;
But good San Marco, if he will,
Can save his own fair city still.
   I put my trust in him.'

VII.

"So—for the night was closing o'er—
   San Marco's Riva by,
I thought my little boat to moor,
   And lie down patiently
To sleep, or watch, as best I might,
Telling my beads till morning light—
I scarce could see to make all tight,
   Night fell so suddenly.

VIII.

"While I still fumbled, stooping low,
   A voice hailed close at hand.
I started to my feet, and lo!
   Hard by, upon the strand,
Stood one in close-cowled garments white,
Who seemed by that uncertain light,
Methought, an holy Carmelite,
   Slow beckoning with the hand.

IX.

"Before, in answer to the call,
   I'd cleared my husky throat,
Down leapt that stately form and tall
   Into my crazy boat—
A weight to crush it through. But no,
He came down light as feathered snow,
As soundless; and, composedly
Taking his seat, 'My son,' said he,
   'Unmoor and get afloat.'

X.

"'Corpo di Bacco! get afloat
   In such a storm!' quoth I,

'Just as I'm mooring my old boat
  Here snug all night to lie.
And, Padre, might I make so free,
What service would you have of me?'
'First to San Giorgio,' answered he,
  'Row swift and steadily;

XI.

"'And fear thou not; for a strong arm
  Will be with thee,' he said,
'And not a hair shall come to harm,
  This night, of thy grey head.
And guerdon great shall be thy meed,
If faithful thou art found at need.'
'Well, good San Marco be my guide,'
Quoth I, and my old boat untied;
  'I've little cause for dread:

XII.

"'Nothing to lose but my old life,—
  So for San Giorgio!—hey!'
Never again so mad a strife
  Unto my dying day
Shall I e'er wage with wind and sea;
And yet we danced on merrily:
Now cleaving deep the briny grave,
Now breasting high the foamy wave,
  Like waterfowl at play.

XIII.

"How we spun on! 'Tis true I plied
  That night a lusty oar;
But such a wind and such a tide
  Down full upon us bore!

And yet—in marvellous little space
We reached San Giorgio's landing-place.
'Well so far,' said my ghostly fare,
And bidding me await him there,
   Rose up, and sprang ashore.

XIV.

"And in a moment he was gone,
  Lost in the dark profound;
Nor, as my oars I lay upon,
  Heard I a footfall sound
Going or coming; and yet twain
Stood there when the voice hailed again,
  And, starting, I looked round.

XV.

"Down stept they both into the boat—
  'And now, my son,' said he
Whom first I took—'once more afloat,
  Row fast and fearlessly;
And for San Nicolo make straight.'
  'Nay, nay,' quoth I—''tis tempting fate;'
But he o'erruled me, as of late,
  And—splash!—away went we.

XVI.

"Away, away—through foam and flood!
  'Rare work this same!' thought I,
'Yet, faith, right merrily we scud;
  A stouter oar I ply,
Methinks, than thirty years ago.
The Carmelite keeps faith, I trow—
Hurra, then, for San Nicolo!
  We're a holy crew surely!'

XVII.

"Thus half in jest, half seriously,
    Unto myself I said,
Looking askance at my company.
    But our second trip was sped;
And there, on the marge of the sea-washed strand,
Did another ghostly figure stand,
And down into the boat stept he.
I crossed myself right fervently,
    With a sense of creeping dread.

XVIII.

"But the Carmelite—(I call him so,
    As he seemed at first to me)—
Said, 'Now, my son, for the Castles row!
    Great things thou soon shalt see.'
Without a word, at his bidding now
For the Lido Strait I turned my prow,
And took to my oar with a thoughtful brow,
    And pulled on silently.

XIX.

"When to the Lido pass we came,
    Cospetto! what a sight!
Air, sky, and sea seemed all on flame,
    And by that lurid light
I saw a ship come sailing in
Like a ship of hell, and a fiendish din
From the fiendish crew on her deck rose high,
And 'Ho! ho! ho!' was the cursed cry—
    'Venice is doomed to-night!'

XX.

"Then in my little boat, the three,
  With each a stretched-out hand,
Stood up;—and that sign, made silently,
  Was one of high command.
For in a moment, over all,
Thick darkness dropt, as 'twere a pall;
And the winds and waves sank down to sleep,
Though the muttering thunder, low and deep,
  Ran round from strand to strand.

XXI.

"As it died away, the murky veil,
  Like a curtain, aside was drawn;
And lo! on the sea lay the moonlight pale,
  And the demon-ship was gone.
The moonlight lay on the glassy sea,
And the bright stars twinkled merrily,
  Where the rippling tide rolled on.

XXII.

"'Well done, well done, so far, my son!'
  Said the first of the ghostly three.
'Thy good night's work is wellnigh done,
  And the rich reward to be:
Put back, and, as we homeward row,
Land these my brethren dear; whom know
For San Giorgio and San Nicolo—
  Thou shalt afterwards know me.'

XXIII.

"'And doubtless,' to myself I said,
  'For the greatest of the three:'

But I spoke not; only bowed my head,
    Obeying reverently:
And pulling back, with heart elate,
Landed as bidden my saintly freight.
That ever, old boat, it should be thy fate,
    To have held such company!

XXIV.

"The voyage was done; the Riva won,
    From whence we put to sea.
'And now, my son,' said the mighty one,
    'Once more attend to me.
Present thee with the coming day
Before the Signori, and say,
That I, San Marco, sent thee there,
The great deliverance to declare,
    This night wrought gloriously.

XXV.

"'What thou hast heard and seen this night
    With fearless speech unfold:
And thy good service to requite,
    I will to thee be told
Five hundred ducats!' 'Holy saint!'
I meekly asked, with due restraint,
'Will they believe what I shall say,
And count, on his bare word, such pay
    To the fisherman poor and old?'

XXVI.

"'This token give to them,' said he;
    And from his finger drew
The ring, most noble Signori,
    I here present to you.

'Let search in my treasury be made,
'Twill be found missing there,' he said,
    So vanished from my view !"

XXVII.

There ran a whispering murmur round,
    As Gian closed his tale;
And some, still unbelieving, frowned,
    And some with awe grew pale.
Then all, as with one voice cried out,
" Why sit we here in aimless doubt,
The means and place of proof so nigh?
One glance at the holy treasury
    All words will countervail."

XXVIII.

Led by the Doge Gradenigo,
    Set forth the solemn train,
Through arch and column winding slow,
    Till the great church door they gain.
With them the fisherman was led,
Guarded by two; but his old head
He held up high :—" For sure," said he,
" San Marco will keep faith with me,
    And prove his own words plain."

XXIX.

The Proveditore stept on first,
    With high authority;
And at his word, wide open burst
    The saintly treasury;
And holy monks, with signs devout,
Held high the blessed relics out,

And gifts of emperors and kings,
Priceless, inestimable things,
  Displayed triumphantly.

XXX.

Familiar as their beads to them—
  So oft recounted o'er
Each history—was relic, gem,
  And all the sacred store.
But now—"What know ye of this thing?"
The Doge said, holding forth the ring;
  "Have ye seen its like before?"

XXXI.

Short scrutiny sufficed. "Full well
  That ring we know," said they.
"But if taken hence by miracle,
  Or how, we cannot say.
'Tis the same this blessed image wore,
San Marco's self." All doubt was o'er.
"Viva San Marco evermore!"
  Was the deafening roar that day.

XXXII.

What throat than Gian's louder strained
  The exulting sound to swell?
And when the ducats, fairly gained,
  Into his cap they tell,
With promise for San Marco's sake
Like sum a yearly dole to make:
"Viva San Marco!" shouted he;
"Who would not row in such company
  Against all the fiends in hell?"

THE RIVER.

RIVER! River! little River!
  Bright you sparkle on your way,
O'er the yellow pebbles dancing,
Through the flowers and foliage glancing,
  Like a child at play.

River! River! swelling River!
  On you rush o'er rough and smooth—
Louder, faster, brawling, leaping,
Over rocks, by rose-banks sweeping,
  Like impetuous youth.

River! River! brimming River!
  Broad and deep and *still* as Time,
Seeming *still*—yet still in motion,
Tending onward to the ocean,
  Just like mortal prime.

River! River! rapid River!
  Swifter now you slip away;
Swift and silent as an arrow,
Through a channel dark and narrow,
  Like life's closing day.

River! River! headlong River!
  Down you dash into the sea;
Sea, that line hath never sounded,
Sea, that voyage hath never rounded,
  Like eternity.

SUNDAY EVENING.

I SAT last Sunday evening,
    From sunset even till night,
At the open casement, watching
    The day's departing light.

Such hours to me are holy,
    Holier than tongue can tell,
They fall on my heart like dew
    On the parchèd heather-bell.

The sun had shone bright all day—
    His setting was brighter still,
But there sprang up a lovely air
    As he dropt down the western hill.

The fields and lanes were swarming
    With holiday folks in their best,
Released from their six days' cares
    By the seventh day's peace and rest.

I heard the light-hearted laugh,
    The trampling of many feet;
I saw them go merrily by,
    And to me the sight was sweet.

There's a sacred soothing sweetness,
    A pervading spirit of bliss;
Peculiar from all other times,
    In a Sabbath eve like this.

Sunday Evening.

Methinks, though I knew not the day,
   Nor beheld those glad faces, yet all
Would tell me that Nature was keeping
   Some solemn festival.

The steer and the steed in their pastures
   Lie down with a look of peace,
As if they knew 'twas commanded
   That this day their labour should cease.

The lark's vesper song is more thrilling
   As he mounts to bid heaven good-night;
The brook sings a quieter tune,
   The sun sets in lovelier light.

The grass, the green leaves, and the flowers,
   Are tinged with more exquisite hues;
More odorous incense from out them
   Steams up with the evening dews.

So I sat last Sunday evening
   Musing on all these things,
With that quiet gladness of spirit
   No thought of this world brings:

I watched the departing glory,
   Till its last red streak grew pale,
And earth and heaven were woven
   In twilight's dusky veil.

Then the lark dropt down to his mate
   By her nest on the dewy ground;
And the stir of human life
   Died away to a distant sound:

Sunday Evening.

All sounds died away—the light laugh,
    The far footstep, the merry call—
To such stillness, the pulse of one's heart
    Might have echoed a rose-leaf's fall:

And, by little and little, the darkness
    Waved wider its sable wings,
Till the nearest objects and largest
    Became shapeless confusèd things—

And, at last, all was dark—then I felt
    A cold sadness steal over my heart;
And I said to myself, "Such is life!
    So its hopes and its pleasures depart!

"And when night comes—the dark night of age,
    What remaineth beneath the sun
Of all that was lovely and loved?
    Of all we have learnt and done?

"When the eye waxeth dim, and the ear
    To sweet music grows dull and cold,
And the fancy burns low, and the heart—
    Oh, heavens! *can* the heart grow old?

"Then, what remaineth of life
    But the lees with bitterness fraught?
What then?"—But I checked as it rose,
    And rebuked that weak, wicked thought.

And I lifted mine eyes up, and lo!
    An answer was written on high
By the finger of God himself,
    In the depths of the dark blue sky.

There appeared a sign in the east—
A bright, beautiful, fixed star!
And I looked on its steady light
   Till the evil thoughts fled afar;

And the lesser lights of heaven
   Shone out with their pale soft rays,
Like the calm unearthly comforts
   Of a good man's latter days;

And there came up a sweet perfume
   From the unseen flowers below,
Like the savour of virtuous deeds,
   Of deeds done long ago—

Like the memory of well-spent time,
   Of things that were holy and dear;
Of friends, "departed this life
   In the Lord's faith and fear."

So the burden of darkness was taken
   From my soul, and my heart felt light;
And I laid me down to slumber
   With peaceful thoughts that night.

THE CHURCHYARD.

THE thought of early death was in my heart;
   Of the dark grave, and "dumb forgetfulness;"
     And with a weight like lead,
     And overwhelming dread,
Mysteriously my spirit did oppress.

The Churchyard.

And forth I roamed in that distressful mood
  Abroad into the sultry, sunless day;
    All hung with one dark cloud,
    That like a sable shroud
On Nature's deep sepulchral stillness lay.

Black fell the shadows of the churchyard elms—
  Unconsciously my feet had wandered there—
    And through that awful gloom—
    Head-stone and altar tomb
Among the green heaps gleamed with ghastlier glare.

Death—death was in my heart, as there I stood,
  Mine eyes fast fixed upon a grass-grown mound;
    As though they would descry
    The loathsome mystery
Consummating beneath that charnel ground.

Death—death was in my heart. Methought I felt
  A heavy hand, that pressed me down below;
    And some resistless power
    Made me, in that dark hour,
Half long *to be*, where I abhorred to go.

Then suddenly, albeit no breeze was felt,
  Through the tall tree-tops ran a shivering sound—
    Forth from the western heaven
    Flashed out the flaming levin,
And one long thunder-peal rolled echoing round.

One long, long echoing peal, and all was peace;
  Cool rain-drops gemmed the herbage—large and few;
    And that dull vault of lead,
    Disparting over head,
Down beamed an eye of soft celestial blue.

And up toward the heavenly portal sprang
  A skylark, scattering off the feathery rain—
    Up from my very feet;—
    And oh! how clear and sweet
  Rang through the fields of air his mounting strain.

Blithe, blessed creature! take me there with thee—
  I cried in spirit—passionately cried—
    But higher still and higher
    Rang out that living Lyre,
  As if the Bird disdained me in his pride.

And I was left below, but now no more
  Plunged in the doleful realms of Death and Night—
    Up with the skylark's lay,
    My soul had winged her way
  To the supernal source of Life and Light.

———o———

TO THE SWEET-SCENTED CYCLAMEN.

I LOVE thee well, my dainty flower!
  My wee, white cowering thing,
That shrinketh like a cottage maid,
Of bold, uncivil eyes afraid,
  Within thy leafy ring!

I love thee well, my dainty dear!
  Not only that thou'rt fair—
Not only for thy downcast eye,
Nor thy sweet breath, so lovingly
  That woos the caller air—

To the Sweet-Scented Cyclamen.

But that a world of dreamy thoughts
    The sight of thee doth bring;
Like birds who've wandered far from hence,
And come again, we know not whence,
    At the first call of spring.

As here I stand and look on thee,
    Before mine eyes doth pass—
Clearing and quickening as I gaze—
An evening scene of other days,
    As in a magic glass.

I see a small old-fashioned room,
    With pannelled wainscot high—
Old portraits, round in order set,
Carved heavy tables, chairs, buffet
    Of dark mahogany;

Twin china jars, on brackets high,
    With grinning Monsters crowned;
And one that, like a Phœnix' nest,
Exhales all Araby the Blest,
    From that old bookcase round.

And there a high-backed, hard settee,
    On six brown legs and paws,
Flowered o'er with silk embroidery,
And there, all rough with filigree,
    Tall screens on gilded claws.

Down drops the damask curtain there
    In many a lustrous fold;
The fire-light flashing broad and high,
Floods its pale amber gorgeously
    With waves of redder gold.

To the Sweet-Scented Cyclamen.

And lo! the flamy brightness wakes
    Those pictured shapes to life—
My Lady's lip grows moist and warm,
And dark Sir Edward's mailèd form
    Starts out for mortal strife;

And living, breathing forms are round—
    Some gently touched by Time,
Staid Elders, clustering by the hearth,
And *one*, the soul of youthful mirth,
    Outlasting youthful prime.

And there—where *she* presides so well,
    With fair dispensing hands—
Where tapers shine, and porcelain gleams,
And muffins smoke, and tea-urn steams,
    The Pembroke Table stands—

That heir-loom Tea-pot—Graphic Muse!
    Describe it if thou'rt able—
Methinks—were such advances meet—
On those three, tiny, toddling feet,
    'Twould swim across the table

And curtsy to the coffee-pot—
    Coquettishly demure,—
Tall, quaint compeer!—fit partner he
To lead with her so gracefully
    Le minuét de la cour!

Ah, precious Monsters! dear Antiques!
    More beautiful to me,
Than modern, fine, affected things,
With classic claws, and beaks, and wings—
    "God save the mark!"—can be.

To the Sweet-Scented Cyclamen.

How grateful tastes the infusèd herb!
　　How pleasant its perfume!
Some sit and sip;—with cup in hand
This saunters round;—while others stand
　　In knots about the room—

In cozy knots—there, three and four—
　　And here, one, two, and three—
Here by my little dainty flower—
Oh fragrant thing! Oh pleasant hour!
　　Oh gentle company!

Come, Idler, set that cup aside,
　　And tune the flute for me—
What will I have? Oh, prithee, play
That air I love—" Te bien aimer
　　Pour toujours ma Zelie."

Sweet air!—sweet flower!—sweet social looks!—
　　Dear friends!—young, happy hearts!
How now!—What! all alone am I?
Come they with cruel mockery
　　Like shadows to depart?

Ay, shadows all—gone every face
　　I loved to look upon—
Hushed every strain I loved to hear,
Or sounding in a distant ear—
　　" All gone!—all gone!—all gone!"

Some far away in other lands—
　　In this, some worse than dead—
Some in their graves laid quietly—
One, slumbering in the deep, deep sea—
　　All gone!—all lost!—all fled!

And here am I—I live and breathe,
    And stand, as *then* I stood,
Beside my little dainty flower—
But *now*, in what an altered hour!
    In what an altered mood!

And yet I love to linger here—
    To inhale this odorous breath,
Faint as a whisper from the tomb—
To gaze upon this pallid bloom
    As on the face of Death.

THE WELCOME HOME.—1820.

HARK! hark! they're come!—those merry bells,
    That peal their joyous welcome swells;
And many hearts are swelling high,
With more than joy—with ecstasy!

And many an eye is straining now
T'ward that good ship, that sails so slow;
And many a look toward the land
They cast, upon that deck who stand.

Flow, flow, ye tides!—ye languid gales,
Rise, rise, and fill their flagging sails!—
Ye tedious moments, fly, begone,
And speed the blissful meeting on.

Impatient watchers! happy ye,
Whose hope shall soon be certainty;
Happy, thrice happy! soon to strain
Fond hearts to kindred hearts again!

The Welcome Home.

Brothers and sisters—children—mother—
All, all restored to one another!
All, all returned!—And are there none
To me restored, returned?—Not one.

Far other meeting mine must be
With friends long lost—far other sea
Than thou, oh restless ocean! flows
Betwixt us—One that never knows

Ebb-time or flood;—a stagnant sea;—
Time's gulf;—its shore Eternity!—
No voyager from that shadowy bourne
With chart or sounding may return.

There, there they stand—the loved!—the lost!
They beckon from that awful coast!—
They cannot thence return to me,
But I shall go to them.—I see

E'en now, methinks, those forms so dear,
Bend smiling to invite me there.—
Oh! best beloved! a little while,
And I obey that beckoning smile!

'Tis all my comfort now, to know
In God's good time it shall be so;
And yet, in that sweet hope's despite,
Sad thoughts oppress my heart to-night.

And doth the sight of others' gladness
Oppress this selfish heart with sadness?
Now Heaven forbid!—but tears will rise—
Unbidden tears—into mine eyes.

The Welcome Home.

When busy thoughts contrast with theirs
My fate, my feelings—Four brief years
Have winged their flight, since, where they stand,
I stood and watched that parting band

Then parting hence—and one, methought—
Oh, human foresight! set at nought
By God's unfathomed will!—was borne
From England, never to return!—

With saddened heart I turned to seek
Mine own belovèd home—to speak
With her who shared it, of the fears
She also shared in . . . . It appears

But yesterday that thus we spoke;
And I can see the very look
With which she said, "I do believe
Mine eyes have ta'en their last long leave

Of her who is gone hence to-day!"
Five months succeeding slipped away;
And, on the sixth, a deep-toned bell
Swung slow, of recent death to tell!

It tolled for her, with whom so late
I reasoned of impending fate;
To me, those solemn words who spoke
So late with that remembered look!

And now, from that same steeple, swells
A joyous peal of merry bells,
Her welcome, whose approaching doom
We blindly thought—a foreign tomb!

THE DEATH OF THE FLOWERS.

HOW happily, how happily the flowers die away!
    Oh! could we but return to earth as easily as they;
Just live a life of sunshine, of innocence, and bloom,
Then drop without decrepitude or pain into the tomb.

The gay and glorious creatures! "they neither toil nor spin,"
Yet lo! what goodly raiment they're all apparelled in;
No tears are on their beauty, but dewy gems more bright
Than ever brow of eastern Queen, endiademed with light.

The young rejoicing creatures! their pleasures never pall—
Nor lose in sweet contentment, because so free to all;
The dew, the shower, the sunshine; the balmy blessed air,
Spend nothing of their freshness, though all may freely share.

The happy careless creatures! of time they take no heed;
Nor weary of his creeping, nor tremble at his speed;
Nor sigh with sick impatience, and wish the light away;
Nor, when 'tis gone, cry dolefully, "Would God that it were day."

And when their lives are over, they drop away to rest,
Unconscious of the penal doom, on holy Nature's breast—
No pain have they in dying—no shrinking from decay.
Oh! could we but return to earth as easily as they!

WHEN SHALL WE MEET AGAIN?

"WHEN shall we meet again?" my friend,
    An awful question thine;
"Where shall we meet again?" Not ours
    The secret to divine.

Not ours to lift the veil, perchance
    In tender mercy drawn;
Oh! could we look beyond, would Hope
    Still lead us cheerly on?

Should we behold two living friends,
    Long sundered, meet at last
In the far distance? or appalled,
    Our shuddering glances cast

On a dark mound of Paynim mould
    Uncrowned by turbaned stone;
Or a green grave of English earth,
    As lowly and as lone?

Oh! likelier that—that English grave;
    And one methinks may stand
Hereafter on its sod, and think
    "Alas, my native land!

"A warmer welcome had been mine
    This trying hour to cheer,
Had the poor heart been warm with life
    Which darkly moulders here."

Nay, let it fall, that blessed veil
  Which shuts the future out;
The earthly future—but beyond,
  Away with dread and doubt.

" When shall we meet?" When Time is o'er,
  And sorrow past, and pain;
" Where shall we meet?" God grant, in heaven,
  Never to part again.

THE LANDING OF THE PRIMROSE.

AUSTRALIA'S strand was swarming
  With myriads, tier on tier;
Like bees, they clung and clustered
  On wall and pile and pier.

The wanderer and the outcast—
  Hope—Penitence—Despair—
The felon and the freeman,
  Were intermingling there.

There ran a restless murmur,
  A murmur deep, not loud;
For every heart was thrilling
  Through all that motley crowd;

And every eye was straining
  To where a good ship lay,
With England's red-cross waving
  Above her decks that day.

The Landing of the Primrose.

And comes she, deeply freighted
   With human guilt and shame?
And wait those crowds expectant
   To greet with loud acclaim?

Or comes she treasure-laden,
   And ache those anxious eyes
For sight of her rich cargo,
   Her goodly merchandise?

See, see! they lower the long-boat,
   And now they man the barge;
Tricked out and manned so bravely
   For no ignoble charge.

Gold gleams on breast and shoulder
   Of England's own true-blue;
That sure must be the captain
   Salutes his gallant crew;

And that the captain's lady
   They're handing down the side;
"Steady, my hearts, now, steady!"
   Was that the coxswain cried.

"Hold on!"—she's safely seated;
   "In oars!"—a sparkling splash;
"Hats off on deck!"—one cheer now;
   "Pull hearties!"—off they dash.

And now the lines long stretching
   Of earnest gazers strain,
Converging to one centre,
   The landing-place to gain.

The Landing of the Primrose.

"A guard! a guard!" in haste then
  The governor calls out;
"Protect the lady's landing
  From all that rabble rout."

Her foot is on the gunwale,
  Her eyes on that turmoil;
A moment so she lingers,
  Then treads Australia's soil.

With looks of humid wonder
  She gazes all about;
And oh! her woman's nature
  Calls that no "*rabble rout.*"

For well she reads the feeling
  Each face expressive wears;
And well she knows what wakes it—
  That precious thing she bears.

That precious thing—oh, wondrous!
  A spell of potent power
From English earth transported,
  A little lowly flower.

Be blessings on that lady,
  Be blessings on that hand,
The first to plant the primrose
  Upon the exile's land!

The sound had gone before her,
  No eye had closed that night;
So yearned they for the morrow,
  So longed they for the light.

The Landing of the Primrose.

She smiles while tears are dropping,
   She holds the treasure high;
And land and sea resounding,
   Ring out with one wild cry.

And sobs at its subsiding
   From manly breasts are heard,
Stern natures, hearts guilt-hardened,
   To woman's softness stirred.

One gazes all intentness—
   That felon boy—and lo!
The bold bright eyes are glistening,
   Long, long unmoistened so.

The woman holds her child up:
   "Look, little one!" cries she,
"I pulled such when as blithesome
   And innocent as thee."

No word the old man utters,
   His earnest eyes grow dim;
One spot beyond the salt sea
   Is present now to him.

There blooms the earliest primrose,
   His father's grave hard by;
There lieth all his kindred—
   There he shall never lie.

The living mass moves onward,
   The lady and her train;
They press upon her path still,
   To look and look again.

Yet on she moves securely,
  No guards are needed there;
Of her they hem so closely
  They would not harm a hair.

Be blessings on that lady!
  Be blessings on that hand!
The first to plant the primrose
  Upon the exile's land.

THE DYING MOTHER TO HER INFANT.

MY Baby! my poor little one! thou'rt come a winter flower,
A pale and tender blossom, in a cold unkindly hour;
Thou comest like the snowdrop, and like that pretty thing,
The power that calls my bud to life will shield its blossoming.

The snowdrop hath no guardian leaves, to fold her safe and warm,
Yet well she bides the bitter blast, and weathers out the storm;
I shall not long enfold thee thus—not long, but well I know
The everlasting arms, my Babe! will never let thee go.

The Dying Mother to her Infant.

The snowdrop—how it haunts me still!—hangs down her
    fair young head;
So thine may droop in days to come, when I have long
    been dead.
And yet the little snowdrop's safe—from her instruction
    seek;
For who would crush the motherless, the lowly and the
    meek?

Yet motherless thou'lt not be long—not long in name, my
    life!
Thy father soon will bring him home another, fairer wife;
Be loving, dutiful to her—find favour in her sight,
But never, O my child, forget thine own poor mother
    quite.

But who will speak to thee of her?—the gravestone at her
    head
Will only tell the name and age and lineage of the dead;
But not a word of all the love—the mighty love for thee,
That crowded years into an hour of brief maternity.

They'll put my picture from its place, to fix another's there,
That picture that was thought so like, and then so passing
    fair!
Some chamber in thy father's house they'll let thee call
    thine own;
Oh! take it there to look upon, when thou art all alone—

To breathe thine early griefs unto, if such assail my child;
To turn to from less loving looks, from faces not so mild.
Alas! unconscious little one, thou'lt never know that best,
That holiest home of all the earth, a living Mother's breast.

The Dying Mother to her Infant.

I do repent me now too late of each impatient thought,
That would not let me tarry out God's leisure as I ought:
I've been too hasty, peevish, proud; I longed to go away;
And now I'd fain live on for thee, God will not let me stay.

Oh! when I think of what I was, and what I might have been,—
A bride last year—and now to die!—and I am scarce nineteen:
And just—just opening in my heart a fount of love so new!
So deep!—Could that have run to waste—could that have failed me too?

The bliss it would have been to see my daughter at my side!
My prime of life scarce overblown, and hers in all its pride.
To deck her with my finest things—with all I've rich and rare;
To hear it said—" How beautiful! and good as she is fair!"

And then to place the marriage wreath upon that bright young brow—
Oh! no—not that—'tis full of thorns——Alas! I'm wandering now.
This weak, weak head! this foolish heart! they'll cheat me to the last:
I've been a dreamer all my life, and now that life is past.

Thou'lt have thy father's eyes, my child!—oh! once how kind they were!
His long black lashes—his own smile—and just such raven hair.

But here's a mark—poor innocent! he'll love thee for't the less—
Like that upon thy mother's cheek his lips were wont to press.

And yet—perhaps I do him wrong—perhaps, when all's forgot
But our young loves, in memory's mood he'll kiss this very spot;
Oh! then, my dearest! clasp thine arms about his neck full fast,
And whisper that I blessed him now, and loved him to the last.

I've heard that little infants converse by smiles and signs
With the guardian band of angels that round about them shines,
Unseen by grosser senses;—belovèd one! dost thou
Smile so upon thy heavenly friends, and commune with them now?

And hast thou not one look for me? Those little restless eyes
Are wandering, wandering, everywhere, the while thy Mother dies;—
And yet—perhaps thou'rt seeking me—expecting me, mine own!
Come, Death! and make me to my child at least in spirit known.

THE LAST JOURNEY.

[Michaud, in his description of an Egyptian funeral procession, which he met on its way to the cemetery of Rosetta, says—" The procession we saw pass stopped before certain houses, and sometimes receded a few steps. I was told that the dead stopped thus before the doors of their friends to bid them a last farewell, and before those of their enemies to effect a reconciliation before they parted for ever."—*Correspondence d' Orient, par* MM. MICHAUD *et* POUJOULAT.]

SLOWLY, with measured tread,
  Onward we bear the dead,
    To his long home.
Short grows the homeward road,
On with your mortal load.
    Oh, Grave! we come.

Yet, yet—ah! hasten not
Past each familiar spot
    Where he hath been;
Where late he walked in glee,
There from henceforth to be
    Never more seen.

Yet, yet—ah! slowly move—
Bear not the form we love
    Fast from our sight—
Let the air breathe on him,
And the sun leave on him
    Last looks of light.

The Last Journey.

Rest ye—set down the bier,
One he loved dwelleth here.
    Let the dead lie
A moment that door beside,
Wont to fly open wide
    Ere he came nigh.

Hearken!—he speaketh yet—
"Oh, friend! wilt thou forget
    (Friend more than brother!)
How hand in hand we've gone,
Heart with heart linked in one—
    All to each other?

"Oh, friend! I go from thee,
Where the worm feasteth free,
    Darkly to dwell—
Giv'st thou no parting kiss?
Friend! is it come to this?
    Oh, friend, farewell!"

Uplift your load again,
Take up the mourning strain!
    Pour the deep wail!
Lo! the expected one
To his place passeth on—
    Grave! bid him hail.

Yet, yet—ah! slowly move;
Bear not the form we love
    Fast from our sight—
Let the air breathe on him,
And the sun leave on him
    Last looks of light.

The Last Journey.

Here dwells his mortal foe;
Lay the departed low,
    E'en at his gate.—
Will the dead speak again?
Uttering proud boasts and vain,
    Last words of hate?

Lo! the dead lips unclose—
List! list! what sounds are those,
    Plaintive and low?
"Oh thou, mine enemy!
Come forth and look on me
    Ere hence I go.

"Curse not thy foeman now—
Mark! on his pallid brow
    Whose seal is set!
Pardoning I passed away—
Thou—wage not war with clay—
    Pardon—forget."

Now his last labour's done!
Now, now the goal is won!
    Oh, Grave! we come.
Seal up this precious dust—
Land of the good and just,
    Take the soul home!

THE SPELL OF MUSIC.

"OH! never, never hand of mine
　　Will wake the harp again,
The viewless harp, the many-voiced,
　　The long beloved in vain.

"Oh! never, never heart of mine,
　　Throughout its inmost core,
With thrilling tones and symphonies
　　Will vibrate as of yore.

"On hand, and heart, and spirit now
　　A deadening spell has dropt—
'The Vision and the Voice' are o'er,
　　The stream of fancy stopt."

'Twas thus I mused, when suddenly
　　A strain of music stole,
Like perfume on the night-breeze borne,
　　Into mine inmost soul.

And lo! the living instrument,
　　The chords unswept so long,
Responded that mysterious touch,
　　And trembled into song.

TOO LATE.

Too late—the curse of life!
  Could we but read
In many a heart the thoughts that inly bleed,
  How oft were found,
Engraven deep, those words of saddest sound,
  Curse of our mortal state,
    Too late! too late!

Tears are there, acrid drops
    That do not rise
  Quick gushing to the eyes,
Kindly relieving, as they gently flow,
    The mitigable woe:
But oozing inward, silent, dark, and chill,
    Like some cavernous rill,
That falls congealing—turning into stone
    The thing it falls upon.

But now and then, maybe,
    The pent-up pain
Breaks out resistless in some passionate strain
    Of simulated grief;
      Seeking relief
      In that fond idle way
From thoughts on life that prey.

"How truthfully conceived!"
    With glistening eyes,
    Some listener cries;

Too Late.

"Fine art to feign so well!"
Ah! none can tell
So truthfully the deep things of the heart
Who have not felt the smart.

Too late—the curse of life!
Take back the cup
So mockingly held up
To lips that may not drain.
Was it no pain
That long heart-thirst?
That the life-giving draught is offered first
On that extremest shore
Who leaves, shall thirst no more.

Take back the cup!—yet, no;
Who dares to say
'Tis mockingly presented? Let it stay.
If here too late,
There is a better state,
A cup that this may typify, prepared
For those who've little of life's sweetness shared,
Nor many flowerets found
On earthly ground;
Yet patiently hold on, awaiting meek
The call of Him they seek—
"Come thou that weepest, yet hast stood the test,—
Come to thy rest."

THE EVENING WALK.

> " Those who have laid the harp aside,
>   And turned to idler things,
> From very restlessness have tried
>   The loose and dusty strings,
> And catching back some favourite strain,
> Run with it o'er the chords again."
>   W. S. LANDOR.

MY lonely ramble yester-eve I took,
   Along that pleasant path that by the brook,
Skirting its flowery margin, winds away
Through fields all fragrant now with new-mown hay.
I could not choose but linger as I went,
A willing idler, with a child's content,
Gathering the wildflowers on that streamlet's edge,
Spared by the mower's scythe, a fringing ledge
Of spiky purple, epilobium tall,
Veronicas, and cuplike coronal
Of golden crowsfoot, waving meadow-sweet,
And wilding rose, that dipt the stream to meet.
And that small brook, so shallow and so clear!
The mother-ewe, without a mother's fear,
Led her young lamb from off the shelving brink,
Firm in the midway stream to stand and drink.
'Twas pleasant, as it dipped and gazed, to see
Its wonder at the watery mimicry,
As here and there, the ripple glancing by,
Imaged an up-drawn foot, a round black eye,
Wide staring, and a nose to meet his own
That seemed advancing from below.   Anon,
From the dark hollow of a little cove,

The Evening Walk.

By an old oak root richly groined above,
Where lay the gathered waters, still and deep,
A vaulted well: e'en thence there seems to peep
A round white staring face, that starts away
As he himself starts back in quick dismay.
Again advancing, with a bolder stare,
He butts defiance. Lo! it meets him there,
And answers threat with threat. He stands at bay,
Perplexed, and ripe for warfare or for play.
Who had not loitered, gazed, and smiled like me,
Pleased with the pretty wanton's antic glee?
And cried "O Nature!" from a thankful heart,
"How graceful and how beautiful thou art!"
But all around me in that pleasant place
Was rife with beauty, harmony, and grace.
The glow of sunset mantled earth and sky,
The evening breeze came softly shivering by,
Laden with incense. 'Mongst the tedded hay,
The fresh-discovered carpet, emerald green,
Outspread its velvet softness,—sight, I ween,
Tempting to wistful gaze of lowing kine,
That in their stale, embrownèd pastures pine,
Loathing and restless, and impatient wait
The tardy opening of that barrier gate.
The mower's whetstone there abandoned thrown;
Silent his whistling scythe—himself was gone;
But gamesome Echo, as he trudged away,
Caught up the burden of his rustic lay;
Then, as the double cadence died remote,
From an old thorn-bush near came dropping out
A sweeter strain, so tremulously low
At first, as if the very soul of woe
Wailed in its music; but that dying close
Melted in air, and on the fall arose

A burst of rapture, swelling clear and strong,
In all the wild exuberance of song.
Methought, as all unseen I hearkened nigh,
The little minstrel sang exultingly—
"Man to his home is gone, and leaveth free
The weary world at last to peace and me."

Peace! peace! but not all peace. E'en there was heard
The voice of mourning: a bereavèd bird
(Ah! piteous contrast to that minstrel blithe)
Hovered about the spot where late the scythe,
Wide sweeping, had to prying eyes revealed
Her lowly nest, so cunningly concealed.
There, by rude hands displaced and scattered, lay
The downy cradle of her young; and they—
The callow nurslings, they with chirpings shrill
And quivering pinions, from her loaded bill
That late received their portions—where are they?
Gone—in close wiry cell to pine away,
Where never parent bird's returning strain
Shall wake them up to life and love again.

So, loitering, lingering, musing as I went,
Homeward at last my devious steps I bent,
Leaving the meadows, by the forest road
That skirts the common. Many a neat abode,
Dwelling of rural industry, I passed,
And little fields and gardens, from the waste
Cribbed, long and narrow. Oh! invidious eye,
That passeth not these poor encroachments by
With look averted, if it may not see
In strictness of judicial trust, or free
To gaze unharmful on the poor man's toil,
That blesseth not the increase of the soil.

The Evening Walk.

Stirring with life was every cottage door:
The humble owner there, his labour o'er,
Stood in the sunset, watching down the west
The round, red orb descending: to his breast
One hugged a little infant: one, with knife
Of clumsy fashion, for the neat goodwife
Wrought some rude implement, or made repair
In the old milking-stool or crazy chair:
One stood intently poring o'er the stye
Where munched his pig, with calculating eye
Measuring its growth, and counting o'er and o'er,
How much the profits of so many score;
And many a one still found some task to do
In his small garden, and performed it too
With cheerful heart, as if such toil were play,
After the heat and burden of the day:
And many a one, as close I passed him by,
Bade me "Good-night" with rustic courtesy—
A homely salutation, that to me
Endeareth evening; seemeth then to be,
So oft I've thought, a kindlier sympathy
'Twixt all God's creatures. Should I reason WHY,
Vain were the attempt. I only feel 'tis so;
Yet one perhaps of deeper search might show
The source whence those mysterious feelings flow.

Is it perchance, as darkness draweth nigh—
Type of the grave, where soon we all shall lie—
And sleep, the type of death, comes stealing on,
When, all our strength and all our cunning gone,
The strongest sinews and the wisest head
Shall lie alike defenceless as the dead?—
Is it that *then*, by some mysterious cause,
Man toward man in closer union draws?—

That then, perhaps, as in the dying hour,
Distinctions fade of rank, and wealth, and power,
And human hearts instinctively confess
The mutual bond of mutual helplessness,
Mutual dependence—ay, of great and small—
On One—the God and Father of us all?

Slowly the straggling cottagers I passed,
Still homeward wending, till I reached at last—
There was I ever wont to stand and gaze—
A lonely dwelling, that in bygone days,
But two years back, or little more, had been
The neatest tenement on Rushbrook Green.
A better sort of cottage, it contained
Two upper rooms, whose windows, lattice-paned,
Peered through the thatch and overhanging leaves
Of a young vine. On one side, from the eaves
Sloped down—addition trim of later date—
A long, low penthouse, oft with heart elate
Eyed by the builder:—" There for sure," said he,
" When winter comes, how snug our cow will be."
And the goodwife, like fashionable wives,
Had her own pin-money. Her straw-roofed hives,
Ranged all a-row against the southern wall,
Yielded in prosperous seasons, at the fall,
Such profits as she spread with honest pride
Before her well-pleased partner. Then, beside,
She had her private treasure, hoarded up
For Christmas holiday; a sparkling cup
Of rich brown mead, a neighbour's heart to cheer
On winter evenings; and throughout the year,
For passing guest, a kindly-proffered treat
Of mild metheglin, mild, and pale, and sweet.

There was no garden kept like Isaac Rae's.
Soon after sunrise in the longest days,
And in the twilight, his hard taskwork done
(His long day's labours in the summer sun),
There might you see him, toiling, toiling on,
Till every fading streak of day was gone.
'Tis true, no garden could with Isaac's vie
Round all the common, crammed so curiously,
And yet so neat and fruitful. Then the *wall*—
For *hedge* it were almost a sin to call
The living rampart—*that* was Isaac's pride;
And there he clipt and clipt, and spied and spied,
That from the quickset line, so straight and true,
No vagrant twig should straggle into view.

There were no children kept like Isaac Rae's,
And he had seven. " Well, my Phœbe says,"
Himself once told me, just three years agone,
Presenting proud his last-born little one,—
" She says—the Lord sends hungry mouths, 'tis true,
But then He sends the meat to fill them too;
For we have never wanted, thanks to Him!
Nor sha'n't, while Isaac Rae has life and limb
To labour for them; nor it sha'n't be said
His children ever broke the parish bread,
Not while the Lord is good to us, and still
Gives me the strength to labour, with the will."

The will continued,—but the strength,—alas!
There came a painful accident to pass.
His master's team—for many years the same
His voice had guided, every horse by name,
Like household dogs, accustomed to obey
Its tones familiar—one unlucky day,

Startled to sudden madness, broke away
From all command; and struggling to restrain
Their headlong progress—struggling all in vain—
His footing failed—he fell—and he was gone—
Right o'er his chest the wheel came crushing on.
And yet he lived and lived. Oh, lingering death!
How terrible thou art, when every breath
Is drawn with painful gasp, and some poor heart,
Of mother, child, or wife, for every start
That shakes the sufferer, feels a deadlier throe—
Feels, as I've heard poor Phœbe say, as though
Each time a drop of blood were wrung from thence.
It was the will of All-wise Providence
That Isaac long should linger in his pain,
Yet never known to murmur or complain,
No, nor to wish the tedious time away,
Was he, while helpless on his bed he lay,
Nor one impatient, fretful word to say,
Helpless and hopeless;—yet, a little space
Hope faintly dawned. In the kind surgeon's face—
A man of kind and Christian heart was he—
The ever-watchful wife was quick to see
A changed expression, but she dared not say
" Is there a hope?" lest it should fade away,
That blessed gleam, and leave her dark once more;
So she was mute, but followed to the door
With asking eyes. He, kindly cautious, said—
" There *is* a chance—but——" so unfinished
Leaving the sentence. 'Tis a cruel task
To look discouragement on eyes that ask
Only for leave to hope,—a hard one, too,
Having permitted hope, to keep in view,
Dashing her timid joy, the spectre fear.
At length they whispered in the poor man's ear

That *he might live.* He only shook his head.
But when a low consulting reached his bed
About the county hospital—how there
Patients were treated with the kindest care—
How all that medicine, all that skill could do,
Was done for them—and how they were brought through
The tedious time of slow recovery,
Better than in their own poor homes could be,—
Then lifted he his feeble voice to say,
" Send me not there—Oh! send me not away
From my poor home—my true and tender wife
And loving little ones, to end my life
In a strange place, with all strange faces near:
My father and my mother both died here—
Here in this very room in peace they died,
And sleep in our own churchyard side by side;
And I shall soon be with them where they lie;
Send me not hence, in a strange place to die;
I shall not linger long—'twill soon be past—
Oh! let me see my children to the last."

He had his wish—they sent him not away;
So there upon his own poor bed he lay
Yet a few weeks, awaiting his release,
And there at last he closed his eyes in peace:
In *Christian peace* he yielded up his breath;
But oh! *for him* there *was* a sting in death—
His wife!—his little ones!—and they were seven,
All helpless infants. . . . But for trust in Heaven,
Trust in *His* word who sayeth, " Leave to me
Thy fatherless children," great assuredly
The dying father's parting pang had been.
I saw the widow ere the closing scene,

The funeral, was over.   There she sate
('Twas on a Sabbath morning), calm, sedate,
Composed, and neat, as she had ever been
On the Lord's Day, when I so oft had seen
Her and her husband, and their eldest three,
Hastening to church ; and now prepared was she
And her seven orphans, all in decent show
Of humble mourning, that same path to go,
Following the father's coffin.   They were there,
The little creatures! huddling round her chair,
Troubled and mute, with eyes upon her face
(Some tearful) fixed, and all as if to trace
Its meekly mournful meaning—all save he,
The youngest Innocent: upon her knee
He clambered up, and crowed with baby glee,
And stroked her face, and lisped his father's name.
Then might be seen, convulsive through her frame,
A universal shudder.   Nor alone
Struck to her heart the call.   A wailing moan
Among the elder orphans rose, and one—
The boy of whom his father was so proud—
Fell on his mother's neck, and wept aloud.
Her eyes were misty, but no tears she shed,
Kissing with quivering lips the boy's fair head,
As on her breast, the face concealed, it lay.
And then, to all around, who came to pay—
Neighbours and friends—to the respected dead
Their last sad tribute, some few words she said
Of thankfulness to each, and spoke of *him*
Calmly, while many an eye with tears grew dim.

The funeral moved ; and through the humble door
He passed, who left it to return no more.
Against the side part, as 'twas carried by,

The Evening Walk.

They jarred the coffin; then a stifled cry
Escaped the widow, and a sign, as though
From that insensate form to ward the blow
She felt upon her heart. A moment all
In silence stopt, while one arranged the pall;
Then sounded slow the bearers' heavy tread,
As to his last long home they bore the dead.

The staff and stay of all the house was gone,
And evil days came darkly hurrying on;
And yet with all the energy of love—
A widowed mother's!—that lone woman strove
(The poor have little leisure for their grief)
To feed her little ones without relief
Of parish pittance. "He would grieve," she thought,
"To know his wife and babes so low were brought.
The hand is cold that toiled for us, 'tis true;
But I can still work hard; and Jemmy too
Grows helpful, and he'll earn a trifle soon
T'ward his own keep. The cottage is our own.
And for the garden . . . I can dig there now,
Though not like him indeed. And then our cow——"
But then she stopt and sighed. Alas! she knew
There was a heavy debt, contracted too
To a hard creditor, of whom 'twas known
That he severely reckoned for his own.
"But then," thought she, "it may not all be true
Folks tell of him; and when I humbly sue
Only for patience—for a longer day,
He will not take my children's bread away."
Thou hadst to learn sad truth, poor simple one!
How ten times harder than the hard flint stone
That human heart may be whose god is gold.
The prayer was spurned—the widow's cow was sold.

That stroke fell heavy, but it crushed not quite
The noble spirit that still kept in sight
Its faithful purpose. "All's not gone," she said;
"Their father's words upon his dying bed
Were—'Phœbe, keep them from the workhouse walls
Whilst thou hast strength. There's not a sparrow falls
But *One* above takes note thereof; and He
Will not forsake thy little ones and thee.'"

So she strove on; yea, morning, noon, and night;
For the late traveller oft observed a light,
As o'er the moorland waste he looked afar,
From Phœbe's cottage, twinkling like a star
Athwart the darkness. And I've heard one tell—
One in her prosperous days who knew her well,
An old wayfaring man, whose lonely road,
Oft after midnight, past her poor abode,
Led to the village inn—I've heard him say,
How many a time when he has passed that way
At that dead hour, attracted by the ray
Of her small candle, he has looked within,
And seen her, with a hand all pale and thin,
Plying her needle. "Ay, *so thin*," said he,
"As 'twas held up between the light and me,
Through it the flame with ruddy brightness shone;
And her poor face!—so sharp with care 'twas grown,
The brow so wrinkled, one could scarce have known
'Twas that same face so fair to look upon,
The pleasant comely face of Phœbe Rae.
Once," he continued, "when a deep snow lay
On all the country, one cold winter's night,
I passed her cottage casement, whence the light
Shone forth, but with a dull and fitful flare;
And when I looked within, a dying glare

Flamed from its long, bent wick, but not a spark
Lived on the hearth, where all was cold and dark.
Yet there beside, in her accustomed place,
The widow sat; upon her arms her face,
Fallen forward on the table, where had dropt
Her work, when the relaxing fingers stopt
Benumbed with cold. She slept the heavy sleep
Of one who desperately has striven to keep
O'erwearied nature from her needful rest,
Then all at once gives way. I did my best,
Gently awaking, to revive and cheer
The drooping spirit; but her pain lay *here*"
(Striking his breast). "Nor mine the power to give
A cordial that had made her hope and live.
I could not say—' Poor soul! thy sorrows cease—
Thy children shall have bread—thy sick heart peace.'
But she has peace at last, and they have bread;
The parish feeds them, and her weary head
Lies by her husband's."
      Honest Adam Bell!
The old man loved those simple peasants well,
Whose chronicler he was, whose board had fed,
Whose humble roof had sheltered his grey head,
Whose hearth had warmed him, and whose babes had
  clung
About his neck, with fondly stammering tongue
Lisping old Adam's name. Too true he said.—
The cottage now is all untenanted;
The din of childish mirth resounds no more—
Heart-cheering music—from the humble door;
Closed is the door, and closed the casements all—
There long unanswered may the traveller call;
Creaks the loose vine, down straggling from the wall;
And through the thatch, with vegetation green,

s

House-leek and moss, are the rude rafters seen;
Loose on its hinge the garden wicket sways;
The forest colt within the enclosure strays,
Where never yet, since Isaac fenced it round,
Was hoof-print seen; there idle weeds abound—
Nettles, and docks, and couch-grass, matting o'er
The walks and beds that useful produce bore;
And rambling bindweed, with its flowery rings,
Up the young apple-tree tenacious clings,
Strangling the long wild shoots, and thickly winds
Round currant-bush and gooseberry, her vines
Knotting them fast, and dragging to the ground
Their matted heads, with barren verdure crowned.
And lo! poor Isaac's pride, that prickly screen—
What spoiler's hand relentless there hath been?
Alas! neglect, by slower means 'tis true,
But not less sure, the spoiler's work will do.
Strong were the vernal shoots, the shearer's care
Specially needed, but—he was not there.
And while succeeding summer still was young,
High in the straggling sprays the throstle sung,
And through the stems, unsightly bare beneath,
Pushed in the lawless stragglers of the heath.

Such now, so silent and so desolate,
Is Isaac's cottage. At its crazy gate
I linger oft; and yester-even I stayed
Till tender twilight with her stealthy shade
Veiled the red sunset. "Here is peace," said I,
" In man's abode, in earth, in air, and sky;
But the heart shrinketh from this deathlike rest."
I thought upon the skylark's ruined nest,
Upon her prisoned young, their captive lay,
And on the orphan babes of Isaac Rae.

Then from the cottage wall depended still,
A broken hoop, that oft with emulous skill
I'd seen the happy creatures urge along;
And in one corner lay a little prong,
Fashioned for childish hand, a wooden toy,
The father's shaping for his eldest boy.
I said how the loose vine swung to and fro,
Its long stems creaking with a sound of woe;
But round the little casement still remained
A tall blush-rose tree, there by Phœbe trained,
And loose depending o'er the interior gloom,
One pale, dew-sprinkled flower, the first to bloom,
Hung down like weeping beauty o'er the tomb.

I looked and listened. All within, I knew,
Was dark and tenantless; yet thence stole through
A sound of life and motion; something stirred
The light leaves of the rose, and a small bird
From the dusk chamber, through a broken pane,
Flew forth to light and the fresh fields again.
"Art thou," thought I, "sole tenant of the cot?
Innocent creature! thou profanest not
What once was the abode of innocence
Scarcely less pure than thine."
                             As if with sense
Of that whereon I mused, the bird at hand
On an old mossy pear-tree took his stand,
And dropped his wings, and tuned his little throat
To such a tender, soft, complaining note,
So sweet, so sad, so tremulous, I said,
Surely he mourns the absent and the dead.

"'TIS HARD TO DIE IN SPRING."

" A short time after this he was laid upon his sick-bed, when a bright sun reminded him of his favourite time of year, and he said, 'I shall never see the peach-blossom or the flowers of Spring: it is hard to die in Spring.'
"'God,' he said, 'had placed him in a paradise, and he had everything that could make a man happy.'
"Yet eminently calculated as he was to enjoy such blessings, and nervous as his constitution was, he met the approach of death with composure, with gratitude and resignation to the will of Him whose beneficence had given, and whose pleasure it was now to take away."—
MEMOIRS OF ROBERT SURTEES, ESQ., BY GEO. TAYLOR, ESQ.

"'TIS hard to die in Spring," were the touching words he said,
As cheerfully the light stole in—the sunshine round his bed;
"'Tis hard to die in Spring, when the green earth looks so gay;
I shall not see the peach-blossom."—'Twas thus they heard him say.

'Twas thus the gentle spirit—oh! deem it not offence—
Departing, fondly lingered among the things of sense;
Among the pleasant places where God his lot had cast,
To walk in peace and honour, blessed and blessing to the last.

While some, though heavenward wending, go mourning all their years,
Their meat (so wisdom willeth) the bitter bread of tears,
And some, resisting proudly the soft persuasive word,
Must feel—in mercy made to feel—the terrors of the Lord;

There are whom He leads lovingly, by safe and pleasant
  ways,
Whose service, yea, whose very life, is gratitude and praise—
Diffusive, active, kindly—enjoying to impart—
Receiving to distribute—the service of the heart.

For such this ruined earth all through is not a vale of
  tears,
Some vestige of its primal form amid the wreck appears;
And though immortal longings oft in secret soar above,
The heart awhile contented fills its lower sphere of love.

"God placed me in a paradise!" So spake his grateful
  heart,
As grateful still from all he loved, when summoned to
  depart.
Thrice blessèd he in life and death, to whom, so called,
  'twas given
To pass, before aught faded here, from paradise to heaven!

—o—

LAMENT FOR LILIAS.

IS there no power in love? Hath love no chain
  Of linkèd strength to hold the spirit here?
Has earth no pleasant places to detain
  One heavenly nature from its higher sphere?

Love was about thee, Lilias! from thy birth
  Love, like an atmosphere, encircled thee;

Lament for Lilias.

A flower, almost too beautiful for earth,
   That in our sight did dwell continually.

Our joy, our pride, our darling, our delight!
   More precious in thy sheltering leaves deep set,
That shrinking timidly from common sight,
   Bloomed but for us, our own sweet violet.

But oh! the fragrance that it shed abroad—
   The incense that to highest heaven ascended,
From those meek virtues a heart-searching God
   Loves best, with His dear Son's own meekness blended.

A Stranger came and coveted our flower;
   Yet *not a* Stranger Lilias' heart who won,
And pressed, prevailed, and bore her from her bower,
   To be of his the life, the light, the sun.

Meekly she moved, with matron grace serene,
   In duty and in love's enlargèd sphere;
And the heart blessed her—and the eye was seen
   Warm glistening as her well-known step drew near.

And thus beloved and blessing, was she blessed?—
   So bounteously, that life could have in store
One only gift, which, crowning all the rest,
   Would make her cup of happiness run o'er.

'Twas granted: tidings came—"a child was born:"
   Was there not gladness in the house that day!
Down sank the sun, uprose the merry morn,—
   Pale, cold in death, the new-made mother lay.

Oh! what a ruin—what a wreck was there
Of goodliest structure ever reared below!
Our Best!—our Beautiful as Angels are!—
  Why wouldst thou leave us? Wherefore wouldst
    thou go?

Hadst thou no power, O Love, the fleeting breath
  The life of many lives awhile to stay?
Hast thou no power, O Love! to fight with Death—
  To fight—to overcome—to conquer? Yea,

Thou hast! thou hast! The fight, the victory
  For us, the lost regained, *is* fought and won:
The grave can never hold whom Christ sets free;
  We shall rejoin thee, loved and lovely one!

—o—

THE NIGHT-SMELLING STOCK.

COME, look at this Plant, with its narrow pale leaves,
  And its tall, slim, delicate stem,
Thinly studded with flowers!—yes, with flowers!—There
    they are!
Don't you see at each joint there's a little brown star?
  But, in truth, there's no beauty in them.

So you ask why I keep it, the little mean thing!
  Why I stick it up here, just in sight;—
'Tis a fancy of mine.—" A strange fancy!" you say;

The Night-Smelling Stock.

"No accounting for tastes!"—In this instance you may,
    For the flower . . . . But I'll tell you to-night.

Some six hours hence, when the Lady Moon,
    Looks down on that bastioned wall,
When the twinkling stars dance silently
On the rippling surface of the sea,
    And the heavy night-dews fall;

Then meet me again in this casement niche,
    On the spot where we're standing now.—
Nay, question not wherefore! Perhaps, with me,
To look out on the night, and the broad, bright sea,
    And to hear its majestic flow!

*   *   *   *   *

Well, we're met here again; and the moonlight sleeps
    On the sea, and the bastioned wall;
And the flowers there below—how the night-wind brings
Their delicious breath on its dewy wings!—
    "But there's one," say you, "sweeter than all!"

"Which is it? The myrtle, or jessamine,
    Or their sovereign lady the rose?
Or the heliotrope? or the virgin's bower?
What! neither?"—Oh, no; 'tis some other flower,
    Far sweeter than either of those.

Far sweeter! And where, think you, groweth the plant
    That exhaleth such perfume rare?
Look about, up and down—but take care! or you'll break,
With your elbow, that poor little thing that's so weak.
    . . . . "Why, 'tis *that* smells so sweet, I declare!"

The Night-Smelling Stock.

Ah ha! is it *that?* Have you found out now
 Why I cherish that odd little fright?
"All is not gold that glitters," you know;
And it is not all worth makes the greatest show
 In the glare of the strongest light.

There are human flowers full many, I trow,
 As unlovely as that by your side,
That a common observer passeth by
With a scornful lip, and a careless eye,
 In the heyday of pleasure and pride.

But move one of those to some quiet spot,
 From the mid-day sun's broad glare,
Where domestic peace broods with dove-like wing,
And try if the homely, despisèd thing,
 May not yield sweet fragrance there.

Or wait till the days of trial come—
 The dark days of trouble and woe;
When they shrink, and shut up, late so bright in the sun;—
Then turn to the little despisèd one,
 And see if 'twill serve you so.

And judge not again at a single glance,
 Nor pass sentence hastily:
There are many good things in this world of ours—
Many sweet things and rare—weeds that prove precious flowers—
 Little dreamt of by you or me.

PAST AND PRESENT.

I SAW a little merry maiden,
   With laughing eye and sunny hair,
And foot as free as mountain fairy,
   And heart and spirit light as air.

And hand and fancy active ever,
   Devising, doing, striving still,
Defeated oft, despairing never,
   Up springing strong in heart and will.

I saw her bounding in her gladness
   On a wild heath at dewy morn,
Weaving a glistening wild-rose garland
   With clusters from the scented thorn.

I saw her singing at her needle,
   And quick and well the work went on,
Till song and fingers stopt together,
   Not for sad thought of fair days gone,

But that of fairer still, a vision
   Rose to the happy creature's sight;
And to a fairy world of fancy
   The mind was gone, more swift than light.

I saw her smiling in her slumber,
   The happy day-dream not gone by;
I saw her weep—but bosom sunshine
   Broke out before the tear was dry.

I saw her "troops of friends" encircling,
  Read kind goodwill in many a face,
With a bright glance that seemed exulting:
  O happy world! O pleasant place!

I saw a drooping dark-browed woman,
  With sunken cheek and silvered hair;
The widow's veil more deeply shading
  A shaded brow, the brow of care.

I saw her wandering in her loneness,
  Among the tombs at eventide,
When autumn winds with hollow murmur
  Among funereal branches sighed.

I saw the sere leaves falling round her,
  Where o'er the dead those dark boughs wave.
I heard a voice—I caught a murmur—
  "O weary world! O peaceful grave!"

I thought upon that merry maiden—
  I looked upon that woman lone:
That form so buoyant, this so drooping,
  O Time! O change!—were one—my own.

———o———

THE WINTRY MAY.—1837.

WHEN Summer faded last away
  I sighed o'er every shortening day;
Comparing, with its pale-hued flowers,
My sicklied hopes and numbered hours,
And thinking—"Shall I ever see
That Summer sun renewed for me?"

The Wintry May.

When Autumn shed her foliage sere,
Methought I could have dropt a tear
With every shrivelled leaf that fell,
And frost-nipped blossom. "Who can tell,
When leaves again clothe shrub and tree,"
Whispered my heart, "where thou wilt be?"

But when Old Winter's rule severe
Set in triumphant—dark and drear—
Though shrinking from the bitter blast,
Methought, "This worst once overpast,
With balmy, blessèd Spring, may be
A short revival yet for me."

And this is May—but where, oh! where
The balmy breath, the perfumed air
I pined for, while my weary sprite
Languished away the long, long night,
Living on dreams of roving free
By primrose bank and cowslip lea?

Unkindly season! cruel Spring!
To the sick wretch no balm ye bring;
No herald-gleam of summer days,
Reviving, vivifying rays.
Seasons to come may brighter be,
But Time—Life—Hope—run short with me.

Yet therefore faint not, fearful heart!
Look up and learn "the better part"
That shall outlast Life's little day;
Seek Peace, which passeth not away,
Look to the land where God shall be
Life—light—yea, all in all to thee.

I WEEP, BUT NOT REBELLIOUS TEARS.

I WEEP, but not rebellious tears;
   I mourn, but not in hopeless woe;
I droop, but not with doubtful fears;
   For whom I've trusted, Him I know:
"Lord! I believe, assuage my grief,
And help—oh help mine unbelief!"

My days of youth and health are o'er,
   My early friends are dead and gone;
And there are times it tries me sore
   To think I'm left on earth alone.
But then faith whispers—"'Tis not so;
He will not leave, nor let thee go."

Blind eyes—fond heart—poor soul that sought
   Enduring bliss in things of earth!
Remembering but with transient thought
   Thy heavenly home, thy second birth;
Till God in mercy broke at last
The bonds that held thee down so fast.

As link by link was rent away,
   My heart wept blood, so sharp the pain;
But I have lived to count this day
   That temporal loss eternal gain;
For all that once detained me here
Now draws me to a holier sphere.

A holier sphere, a happier place,
　Where I shall know as I am known,
And see my Saviour face to face,
　And meet, rejoicing round His throne,
The faithful few,* made perfect there
From earthly stain and mortal care.

―o―

"IT IS NOT DEATH."

IT is not Death—it is not Death,
　　From which I shrink with coward fear;
It is, that I must leave behind
　　　　All I love here.

It is not Wealth—it is not Wealth,
　That I am loath to leave behind;
Small store to me—yet all I crave—
　　　　Hath fate assigned.

It is not Fame—it is not Fame,
　From which it will be pain to part;
Obscure my lot—but mine was still
　　　　A humble heart.

---

* The word "few" is used here in no presumptuously exclusive sense of the Author's, but simply as being the Scriptural phrase—"Many are called, but few chosen."

The word having been altered lately, in two religious publications, where the poem was inserted unknown to the Author, it is thought proper to annex this note.

"It is not Death."

It is not Health—it is not Health,
    That makes me fain to linger here;
For I have languished on in pain
             This many a year.

It is not Hope—it is not Hope,
    From which I cannot turn away;
Oh, earthly Hope hath cheated me
             This many a day.

But there are Friends—but there are Friends,
    To whom I could not say, "Farewell!"
Without a pang more hard to bear
             Than tongue can tell.

But there's a thought—but there's a thought,
    Will arm me with that pang to cope;
Thank God! we shall not part like those
             Who have no hope.

And some are gone—and some are gone—
    Methinks they chide my long delay—
With whom, it seemed, my very life
             Went half away.

But we shall meet—but we shall meet,
    Where parting tears shall never flow;
And when I think thereon, almost
             I long to go.

The Saviour wept—the Saviour wept
    O'er him he loved—corrupting clay!—
But then he spake the word, and Death
             Gave up his prey!—

A little while—a little while,
  And the dark Grave shall yield its trust;
Yea, render every atom up
        Of human dust.

What matters then—what matters then
  Who earliest lays him down to rest?—
Nay, "to depart, and be with Christ,"
        Is surely best.

—o—

ABJURATION.

THERE was a time—sweet time of youthful folly!
  Fantastic woes I courted, feigned distress,
Wooing the veilèd phantom Melancholy
  With passion, born, like Love, "in idleness."

And like a lover—like a jealous lover—
  I hid mine idol with a miser's art,
Lest vulgar eyes her sweetness should discover,
  Close in the inmost chambers of mine heart—

And then I sought her—oft in secret sought her,
  From merry mates withdrawn and mirthful play,
To wear away, by some deep stilly water
  In greenwood haunt, the livelong summer day—

Watching the flitting clouds, the fading flowers,
  The flying rack athwart the waving grass;
And murmuring oft, "Alack! this life of ours!—
  Such are its joys—so swiftly doth it pass!"

Abjuration.

And then mine idle tears—ah, silly maiden!—
   Bedropt the liquid grass like summer rain,
And sighs, as from a bosom sorrow-laden,
   Heaved the light heart that knew no real pain.

And then I loved to haunt lone burial-places,
   To pace the churchyard earth with noiseless tread,
To pore in new-made graves for ghastly traces—
   Brown crumbling bones of the forgotten dead ;

To think of passing bells, of dead and dying—
   'Twere good, methought, in early youth to die,
So loved! lamented!—in such sweet sleep lying,
   The white shroud all with flowers and rosemary

Stuck o'er by loving hands!—but then, 'twould grieve me
   Too sore, forsooth! the scene my fancy drew—
I could not bear the thought to die and leave ye;
   And I have lived, dear friends! to weep for you.

And I have lived to prove what "fading flowers"
   Are life's best joys, and all we love and prize—
What chilling rains succeed the summer showers!
   What bitter drops wrung slow from elder eyes!

And I have lived to look on " death and dying,"
   To count the sinking pulse—the shortening breath ;
To watch the last faint life-streak flying—flying ;
   To stoop—to start! to be alone with death!

And I have lived to feign the smile of gladness,
   When all within was cheerless, dark, and cold—

T

Abjuration.

When all earth's joys seemed mockery and madness,
    And life more tedious than "a tale twice told."

And now—and now—pale, pining Melancholy!
    No longer veiled for me your haggard brow
In pensive sweetness, such as youthful folly
    Fondly conceited; I abjure ye now!—

Away! avaunt!—no longer now I call ye,
    "Divinest Melancholy! mild, meek maid!"
No longer may your siren spells enthrall me,
    A willing captive in your baleful shade.

"Give me the voice of mirth, the sound of laughter,
    The sparkling glance of pleasure's roving eye!—
The past is past—avaunt, thou dark hereafter!—
    Come, eat and drink—to-morrow we must die!"

So in his desperate mood the fool hath spoken—
    The fool, whose heart hath said, "There is no God;"
But for the stricken soul—the spirit broken—
    There's balm in Gilead still: the very rod,

If we but kiss it as the stroke descendeth,
    Distilleth oil to allay the inflicted smart,
And "Peace that passeth understanding" blendeth
    With the deep sighing of the contrite heart.

Mine be that holy, humble tribulation—
    No longer "feigned distress, fantastic woe;"
I know my griefs—but then my consolation,
    My trust, and my immortal hopes, I know.

ONCE UPON A TIME.

I MIND me of a pleasant time,
    A season long ago;
The pleasantest I've ever known,
    Or ever now shall know:
Bees, birds, and little tinkling rills,
    So merrily did chime;
The year was in the sweet spring-tide,
    And I was in my prime.

I've never heard such music since
    From every bending spray;
I've never plucked such primroses,
    Set thick on bank and brae.
I've never smelt such violets
    As all that pleasant time
I found by every hawthorn-root—
    When I was in my prime.

Yon moory down, so black and bare,
    Was gorgeous then and gay
With golden gorse—bright blossoming—
    As none blooms now-a-day.
The Blackbird sings but seldom now
    Up there in the old Lime,
Where hours and hours he used to sing—
    When I was in my prime.

Such cutting winds came never then
    To pierce one through and through;
More softly fell the silent shower,
    More balmily the dew.

" I never cast a Flower away."

The morning mist and evening haze,
   Unlike this cold grey rime,
Seemed woven warm of golden air—
   When I was in my prime.

And Blackberries—so mawkish now—
   Were finely flavoured then;
And Nuts—such reddening clusters ripe
   I ne'er shall pull again.
Nor Strawberries blushing bright—as rich
   As fruits of sunniest clime;
How all is altered for the worse
   Since I was in my prime!

"I NEVER CAST A FLOWER AWAY."

I NEVER cast a flower away,
   The gift of one who cared for me—
A little flower—a faded flower—
   But it was done reluctantly.

I never looked a last adieu
   To things familiar, but my heart
Shrank with a feeling almost pain,
   Even from their lifelessness to part.

I never spoke the word "Farewell,"
   But with an utterance faint and broken;
An earth-sick longing for the time
   When it shall never more be spoken.

'A FAIR PLACE AND PLEASANT.

A FAIR place and pleasant, this same world of ours!
Who says there are serpents 'mongst all the sweet
   flowers?
Who says every blossom we pluck has its thorn?
Pho! pho! laugh those musty old sayings to scorn.

If you roam to the tropics for flowers rich and rare,
No doubt there are serpents, and deadly ones, there;
If none but the rose will content ye, 'tis true
You may get sundry scratches, and ugly ones too.

But prythee look there—Could a serpent find room
In that close-woven moss, where those violets bloom?
And reach me that woodbine—you'll get it with ease—
Now, wiseacre! where are the thorns, if you please?

I say there are angels in every spot,
Though our dim earthly vision discerneth them not;
That they're guardians assigned to the least of us all,
By Him who takes note if a sparrow but fall;

That they're aye flitting near us, around us, above,
On missions of kindness, compassion, and love;
That they're glad when we're happy, disturbed at our
   tears,
Distressed at our weaknesses, failings, and fears;

That they care for the least of our innocent joys,
Though we're cozened like children with trifles and toys,
And can lead us to bloom-beds, and lovely ones too,
Where snake never harboured, and thorn never grew.

MY EVENING.

Farewell, bright Sun! mine eyes have watched
    Thine hour of waning light;
And tender twilight! fare-thee-well—
    And welcome star-crowned night!

Pale, serious, silent, with deep spell
    Lulling the heart to rest,
As lulls the mother's low sweet song
    The infant on her breast.

Mine own belovèd hour!—mine own!
    Sacred to quiet thought,
To sacred memories, to calm joys,
    With no false lustre fraught!

Mine own belovèd hour! for now,
    Methinks, with garish day
I shut the world out, and with those
    Long lost, or far away,

The dead, the absent, once again
    My soul holds converse free—
To such illusions, Life! how dull
    Thy best reality!

The vernal nights are chilly yet,
    And cheerily and bright
The hearth still blazes, flashing round
    Its ruddy, flickering light.

My Evening.

"Bring in the lamp——so—set it there,
    Just show its veilèd ray
(Leaving all else in shadowy tone)
    Fallen on my book——and—stay—

"Leave my work by me"—Well I love
    The needle's useful art;
'Tis unambitious—womanly—
    And mine's a woman's heart.

Not that I ply with sempstress rage,
    As if for life or bread;
No, sooth to say—unconsciously
    Slackening the half-drawn thread,

From fingers that, as spell-bound, stop,
    Pointing the needle wrong,
Mine eyes towards the open book
    Stray oft, and tarry long.

"Stop, stop! Leave open the glass-door
    Into that winter bower;"
For soon therein the uprisen moon
    Will pour her silvery shower;

Will glitter on those glossy leaves;
    On that white pavement shine;
And dally with her eastern love,
    That wreathing jessamine.

"Thanks, Lizzy! No; there's nothing more
    Thy loving zeal can do;
Only—oh yes!—that gipsy flower,*
    Set that beside me too."—

    * The night-smelling stock.

"That Ethiop, in its china vase?"—
"Ay, set it here;—that's right.
Shut the door after you."—'Tis done;
I'm settled for the night.

Settled and snug;—and first, as if
The fact to ascertain,
I glance around, and stir the fire,
And trim the lamp again.

Then, dusky flower! I stoop to inhale
Thy fragrance. Thou art one
That wooeth not the vulgar eye,
Nor the broad staring sun;

Therefore I love thee!—Selfish love
Such preference may be;—
That thou reservest all thy sweets,
Coy thing! for night and me.

What sound was that? Ah, Madam Puss!
I know that tender mew—
That meek, white face—those sea-green eyes—
Those whiskers, wet with dew,

To the cold glass—the greenhouse glass—
Pressed closely from without;
Well, thou art heard—I'll let thee in,
Though skulking home, no doubt,

From lawless prowl.—Ah, ruthless cat!
What evil hast thou done?
What deeds of rapine, the broad eye
Of open day that shun?

My Evening.   297

What! not a feather plucked to-night?
  Is that what thou wouldst tell
With that soft pur, those winking eyes,
  And waving tail?—Well, well,

I know thee, friend!—But get thee in,
  By Ranger stretch and doze;
Nay, never growl, old man! her tail
  Just whisked across thy nose.

But 'twas no act premeditate,
  Thy greatness to molest:
Then, with that long luxurious sigh,
  Sink down again to rest;

But not before one loving look
  Toward me, with that long sigh,
Says, "Mistress mine! all's right, all's well!
  Thou'rt there, and here am I!"—

That point at rest, we're still again.
  I on my work intent;
At least, with poring eyes thereon,
  In seeming earnest bent;

And fingers, nimble at their task,
  Mechanically true;
Though heaven knows where, what scenes, the while,
  My thoughts are travelling to!

Now far from earth—now over earth,
  Traversing lands and seas;—
Now stringing, in a sing-song mood,
  Such idle rhymes as these;—

My Evening.

Now dwelling on departed days—
    Ah! that's no lightsome mood;—
On those to come—no longer now
    Through Hope's bright focus viewed.

On that which is—ay, there I pause,
    No more in young delight;
But patient, grateful, well assured,
    "Whatever is, is right!"

And all to be is in His hands—
    Oh, who would take it thence?
Give me not up to mine own will,
    Merciful Providence!

Such thought, when other thoughts, may-be,
    Are darkening into gloom,
Comes to me like the angel shape,
    That, standing by the tomb,

Cheered those who came to sorrow there.—
    And then I see and bless
His love in all that He withholds,
    And all I still possess.

So varied—now with book, or work,
    Or pensive reverie,
Or waking dreams, or fancy flights,
    Or scribbling vein, may be;

Or eke the pencil's cunning craft,
    Or lowly murmured lay
To the according viola—
    Calm evening slips away.

My Evening.

The felt-shod hours move swiftly on,
  Until the stroke of ten—
The accustomed signal—summons round
  My little household. Then,

The door unclosing, enters first
  That aged faithful friend,
Whose prayer is with her master's child
  Her blameless days to end.

The younger pair come close behind;
  But her dear hand alone—
Her dear old hand! now tremulous
  With palsying weakness grown—

Must reverently before me place
  The Sacred Book. 'Tis there—
And all our voices, all our hearts,
  Unite in solemn prayer.

In praise and thanksgiving, for all
  The blessings of the light;
In prayer, that He would keep us through
  The watches of the night.

A simple rite! and soon performed;
  Leaving, in every breast,
A heart more fittingly prepared
  For sweet, untroubled rest.

And so we part.—But not before,
  Dear nurse! a kiss from thee
Imprints my brow. Thy fond good-night!
  To God commending me!

Amen!—and may His angels keep
  Their watch around thy bed,
And guard from every hurtful thing
  That venerable head!

THE PRIMROSE.

I SAW it in my evening walk,
  A little lonely flower!
Under a hollow bank it grew,
  Deep in a mossy bower.

An oak's gnarled root, to roof the cave
  With Gothic fretwork sprung,
Whence jewelled fern, and arum leaves,
  And ivy garlands hung.

And from beneath came sparkling out
  From a fallen tree's old shell,
A little rill, that clipt about
  The lady in her cell.

And there, methought, with bashful pride,
  She seemed to sit and look
On her own maiden loveliness
  Pale imaged in the brook.

No other flower—no rival grew
  Beside my pensive maid;
She dwelt alone, a cloistered nun,
  In solitude and shade.

No sunbeam on that fairy well
  Darted its dazzling light—

Only, methought, some clear, cold star
  Might tremble there at night.

No ruffling wind could reach her there—
  No eye, methought, but mine,
Or the young lamb's that came to drink,
  Had spied her secret shrine.

And there was pleasantness to me
  In such belief. Cold eyes
That slight dear Nature's lowliness,
  Profane her mysteries.

Long time I looked and lingered there,
  Absorbed in still delight—
My spirit drank deep quietness
  In, with that quiet sight.

―――*o*―――

ARCHBISHOP GERSON.

A ROMISH LEGEND.

A VOICE from the sinful city
  Goes up to God on high—
"Why tarries the righteous doom,
When the time of o'erflowing is come
  Of the cup of iniquity?"

And the good Archbishop Gerson,
  As he kneels in penance drear,
On the cold hard flags so white,
At the hour of dead midnight,
  That accusing voice doth hear.

And, groaning, he lifteth up
  His eyes to the holy rood;
When lo! from the piercèd side,
And the gaping nail-wounds wide,
  Wells out as 'twere fresh-drawn blood.

The old man beats his breast,
  At that awful sight, full sore;
And he bends down his aged brow—
All beaded with sweat-drops now—
  Till it toucheth the marble floor.

And he wrestles in earnest prayer;
  But the accusing voice still cries,
"How long, O Lord! how long
Wilt thou bear with *thy* people's wrong—
  With *this* people's iniquities?"

"Haste hither, my brethren dear!
  And humble yourselves with me,
My holy brethren all!"
Is the Archbishop's piercing call,
  In the strength of his agony.

They come at the call with speed,
  They kneel, and weep, and pray;
But the voice of prayer is drowned
In that dread accusing sound,
  "O Lord! make no delay!"

"We are grievous offenders all—
  All leprous and defiled:
What lips shall be found this day
With prevailing prayer to pray,
  Save the lips of a little child?"

Archbishop Gerson.

"Of such little ones hither bring,"
Cries aloud the Archbishop then.
And they gather, at his command,
Round the altar, a sinless band,
   Though the children of sinful men.

And the pure young voices rise
   On the incense of taintless breath:
And there reigneth o'er all the while,
Throughout that majestic pile,
   A stillness as deep as death,

For crozier and cowl alike
   In the dust lie prostrate there;
Of those living men laid low
In the depth of abasement now,
   Stirreth not hand or hair.

But the pleading voice goes up
   From that infant choir the while;
And behold, o'er the face divine
Playeth, like lightning-shine,
   The gleam of a gracious smile.

Then upriseth, like one entranced,
   The Archbishop on his feet:—
"Give thanks for a day of grace!"
He crieth, with radiant face,—
   "Give thanks, as is most meet.

"The Innocents' prayer ascendeth
   Above the Accuser's cry;
Their Angels are heard in heaven,
And a day of grace is given.
   Glory to God most High!"

NOTES TO "THE BIRTHDAY."

(1.) *"To eat and hang,"* p. 69.

There exists, or did exist, in one of the Channel Islands, a singular convivial custom connected with the execution of criminals. The members of Court meet to celebrate the occasion with a dinner, and a few non-professional friends are invited "to come and eat a dead man."

(2.) *"Down to the parish worthies,"* &c., p. 69.

It may be almost superfluous to mention that this line, and, indeed, the whole paragraph, was written previous to the passing of the Municipal Reform Bill.

(3.) *"While the shower,"* p. 72.

"But turn out of the way a little, good scholar, towards yonder high honeysuckle hedge; there we'll sit and sing, whilst this shower falls so gently upon the teeming earth, and gives yet a sweeter smell to the lovely flowers that adorn these verdant meadows. Look, under the broad beech-tree I sat down, when I was last this way a-fishing, and the birds in an adjoining grove seemed to have a friendly contention with an echo, whose dead voice seemed to live in a hollow tree, near to that primrose hill."—ISAAC WALTON.

www.ingramcontent.com/pod-product-compliance
Lightning Source LLC
Chambersburg PA
CBHW022025240426
43667CB00042B/1193